THE FUNDAMENTALS OF
FASHION DRAPING

BASIC BODICE
COWL TOP
CIRCLE SKIRT
BIAS DRESS
KNIT TOP
+ MORE!

NICK VERREOS
DAVID PAUL

Welcome to the World of Fashion Draping!

Draping for Fashion Design is the art of manipulating fabric directly on a dress form, and thus creating a 3-dimensional prototype of a garment. Throughout time, draping has remained a vital component of fashion design and has served as the ideal first step for making a designer's ideas come to life.

In this how-to textbook, you will learn all the fundamentals of Draping for Fashion Design, from proper pinning, marking, and cutting to advanced techniques such as bias draping and trueing your design. In addition, you will find step-by-step instructions on sewing your specific fashion draping assignments including the circle skirt, midriff top, wrap dress, and even a standard knit top.

This illustrated textbook is an essential step-by-step guide for students, up-and-coming fashion designers and fashion design enthusiasts, to learn the fundamental fashion draping techniques that will put you on the path to successfully create the garments you design.

As a Fashion Designers and an instructor of patternmaking & draping with over 25 years of professional experience in the fashion industry, David and I have compiled this book to support and aid beginners in their quest to become proficient in draping and understanding how integral it is to Fashion Design.

XOXO
Nick Verreos

NICK VERREOS

DAVID PAUL

BIOGRAPHY

Nick and David co-founded NIKOLAKI, in 2001. Their collections of upscale red carpet gowns and cocktail dresses have been worn by celebrities such as Beyoncé, Katy Perry, Heidi Klum, Eva Longoria and Carrie Underwood. NIKOLAKI has been carried in over 100 stores across the US and abroad.

Additionally, they design and produce NV Nick Verreos a clothing line which has been available on major Home Shopping Networks including ShopHQ (USA), QVC UK, QVC Italy and The Shopping Channel (Canada).

Nick and David are proud to be the Co-Chairs for the Fashion Design, Advanced Fashion Design, and Film & TV Costume Design Programs at the Fashion Institute of Design & Merchandising/FIDM

NICK VERREOS
Nick was the Winning Mentor of Project Runway: Under the Gunn and first received national and international attention after appearing on Project Runway. He is a red carpet fashion expert and correspondent for various networks including E! Entertainment, KTLA's "LIVE From The Oscars" and ABC's "On The Red Carpet".

Nick received his Bachelor of Arts in Political Science at the University of California, Los Angeles/UCLA. He then continued on to the Fashion Institute of Design & Merchandising/FIDM, where he graduated from the Advanced Fashion Design Program.

As an educator, Nick has been an instructor at FIDM where he taught Fashion Sketching, Draping, Patternmaking and Design.

Nick also shares his knowledge with future fashion designers through his popular YouTube channel, "Fashion School with Nick Verreos," which has over 370,000 subscribers and 11 million views from all over the world.

DAVID PAUL
A Native of Southern California, David Paul earned a Bachelor of Arts in Theater Arts and a Master of Fine Arts Degree in Costume Design from the University of California, Los Angeles/UCLA. He pursued his passion for fashion and costume design, building an impressive career in the entertainment and fashion industries for over two decades.

David designed costumes and worked on popular shows such as "Queer Eye for the Straight Girl", "Passions", "Undressed" and various other productions for MTV, ABC, FOX, NIKELODEON, and the WB. David has also collaborated with renowned figures like Andre Leon Talley and Lisa Love for Vogue Magazine and styled for celebrities including Kate Hudson, Heidi Klum, Vanessa Paradis, Twiggy, and Heather Graham.

TABLE OF CONTENTS

COWL TOP

BIAS SLIP DRESS

KNIT TOP

SCULPTED WRAP DRESS

TERMINOLOGY

DRAPING BASICS

Draping Basics

DO:
When pinning onto the Dress Form or pinning the MUSLIN onto the Dress Form, pin at AN ANGLE, or SLIDE the pin through the Dress Form:

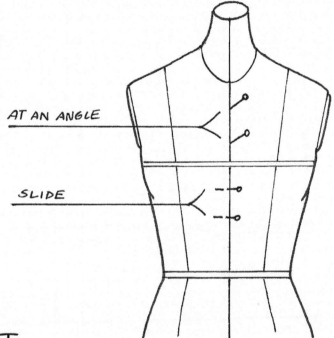

AT AN ANGLE

SLIDE

DON'T:
DO NOT pin STRAIGHT IN; in other words, DO NOT "STAB" the Dress Form:

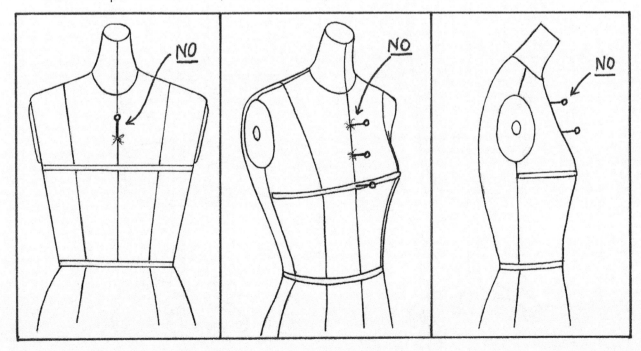

NO

NO

NO

Draping Basics

THE DRESS FORM

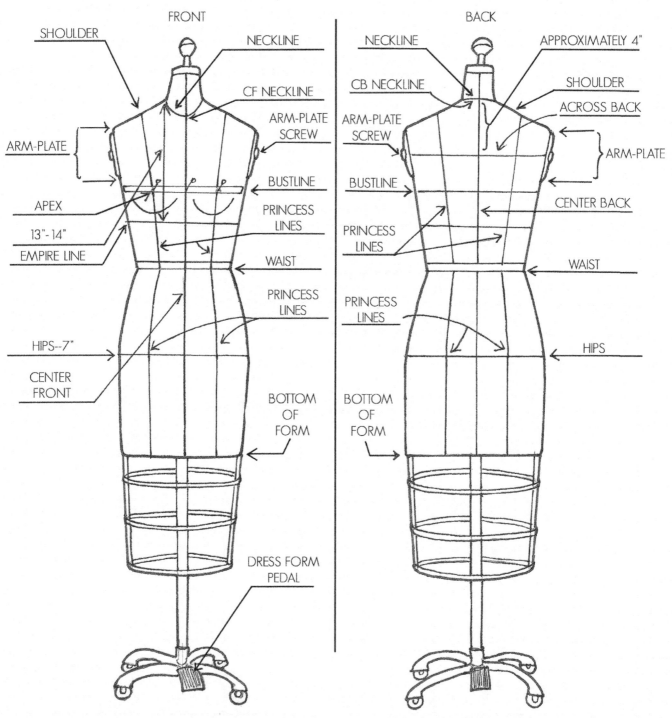

FRONT

BACK

SHOULDER

NECKLINE

CF NECKLINE

ARM-PLATE
SCREW

ARM-PLATE

BUSTLINE

APEX

PRINCESS
LINES

13"-14"

EMPIRE LINE

WAIST

PRINCESS
LINES

HIPS--7"

CENTER
FRONT

BOTTOM
OF
FORM

DRESS FORM
PEDAL

NECKLINE

CB NECKLINE

ARM-PLATE
SCREW

BUSTLINE

PRINCESS
LINES

PRINCESS
LINES

BOTTOM
OF
FORM

APPROXIMATELY 4"

SHOULDER

ACROSS BACK

ARM-PLATE

CENTER BACK

WAIST

HIPS

Draping Basics

THE DRESS FORM

SIDE

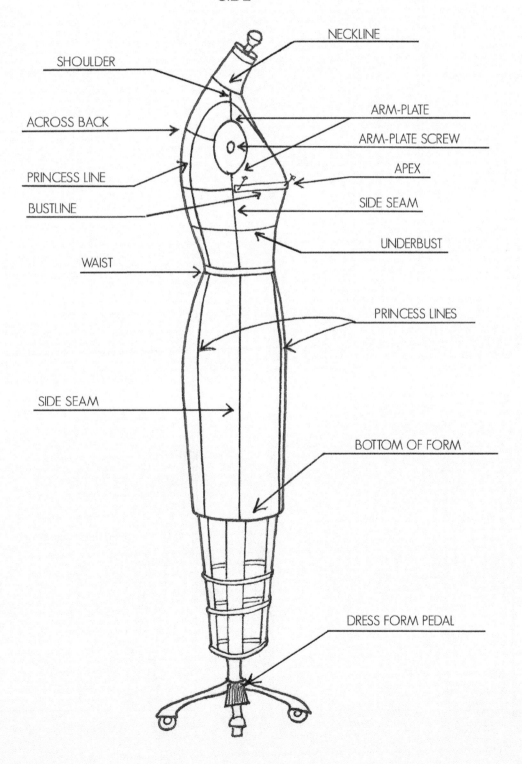

NECKLINE

SHOULDER

ARM-PLATE

ACROSS BACK

ARM-PLATE SCREW

APEX

PRINCESS LINE

SIDE SEAM

BUSTLINE

UNDERBUST

WAIST

PRINCESS LINES

SIDE SEAM

BOTTOM OF FORM

DRESS FORM PEDAL

Draping Basics

MUSLIN

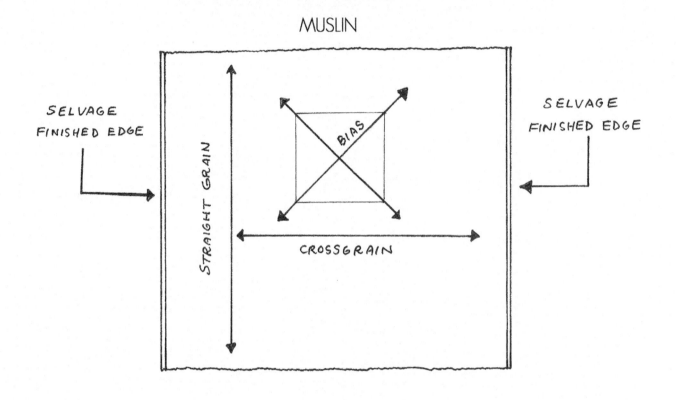

SELVAGE
FINISHED EDGE

SELVAGE
FINISHED EDGE

STRAIGHT GRAIN

BIAS

CROSSGRAIN

BLOCKING

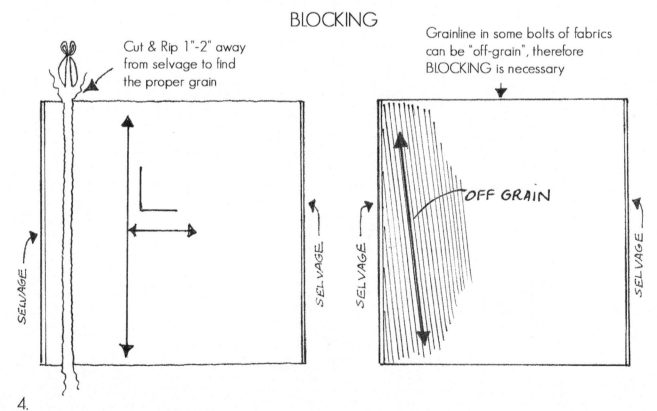

Cut & Rip 1"-2" away
from selvage to find
the proper grain

Grainline in some bolts of fabrics
can be "off-grain", therefore
BLOCKING is necessary

SELVAGE

SELVAGE

OFF GRAIN

SELVAGE

SELVAGE

4.

Draping Basics

PRESSING

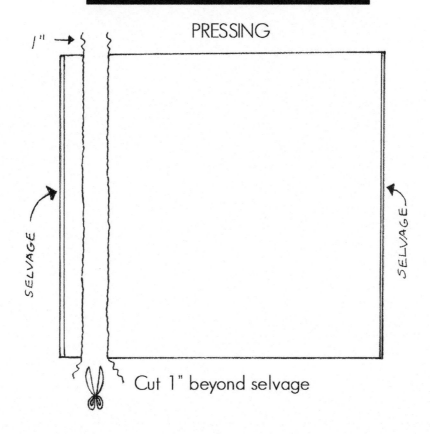

1"

SELVAGE

SELVAGE

Cut 1" beyond selvage

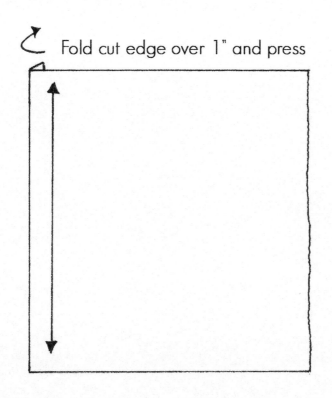

Fold cut edge over 1" and press

BASIC BODICE

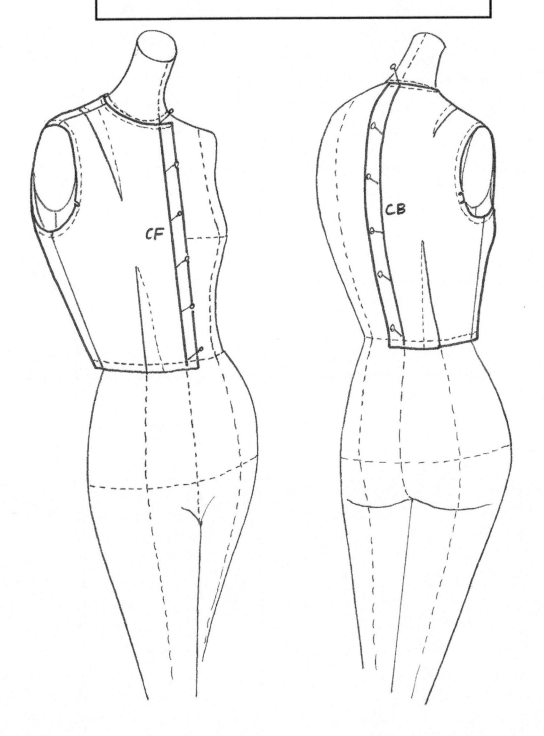

Basic Bodice

2 DART: FRONT & BACK

Start by prepping your Muslin:

    -Cut 2 pieces of Muslin, rectangle shape 25" L x 15" W

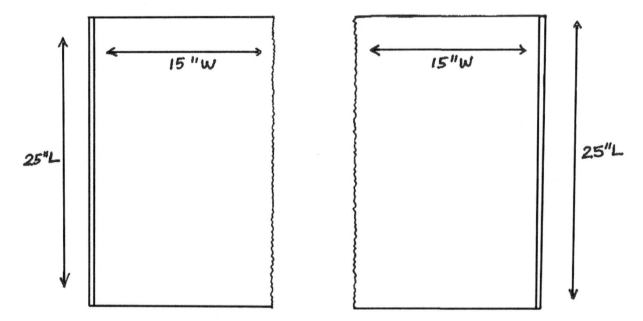

Label one FRONT and label one BACK:

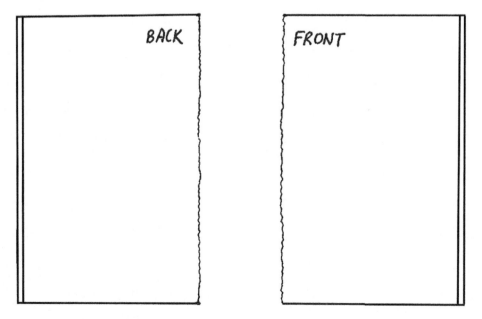

Basic Bodice

2 DART: FRONT & BACK

PRE-DRAPE MARKS:
-Draw CF/Center Front Grainline 1" away from selvage/edge of muslin
-Draw CB/Center Back Grainline 1" away from selvage/edge of muslin
-Press this 1" under to create a fold, and set aside the Back piece.

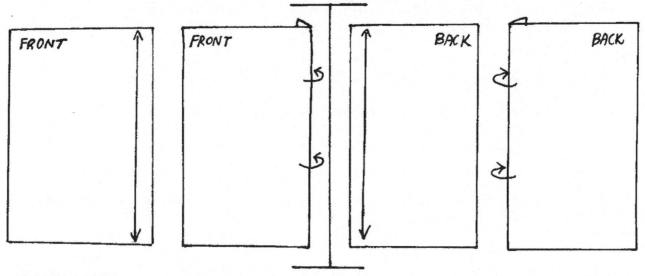

FRONT DRAPE:
1) In the middle of the Front piece of prepped muslin (with 1" fold at CF), draw a perfect crossgrain line using the L-square.
2) Measure CF (center front) to Apex (highest point of bust), mark.
3) Measure Apex to Side Seam, as 1/8" for EASE, then mark.
4) Between Apex and Side Seam marks, draw a straight vertical line to signify middle of side section.

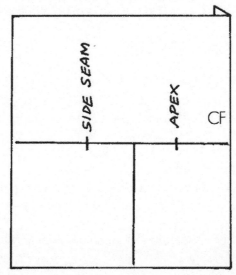

Your Front Basic Bodice Drape Muslin Piece is now PREPPED. Begin Draping!

Basic Bodice

2 DART: FRONT

1.
- Pin the APEX MARK on the fabric to the APEX on the dress form.
- Pin the CF GRAINLINE FOLD of the fabric to the CF position of the dress form.
- Pin at the CF NECK, down CF (at 1"-1 ½" spaced out intervals) and at the WAIST.
- Pin SIDE SEAM at the BUST LEVEL/CROSSGRAIN line
- Pin the FRONT CROSSGRAIN parallel to the floor down the BUSTLINE area.

2.
- Put a pin at the CENTER of the PRINCESS PANEL POSITION at the WAISTLINE on the dress form.
- Pin the WAISTLINE.
- Get rid of excess fabric by trimming the fabric to 2" below the waistline.
- Clip the WAISTLINE fabric at the CENTER of the PRINCESS PANEL as shown.
- Notice excess fabric that is apparent in the PRINCESS area below the BUST (that will be draped into a DART).

3.
- Pin and drape the FRONT WAIST DART using the excess fabric that falls between the CENTER of the PRINCESS PANEL and CF WAIST POSITION.
- Crossmark the PRINCESS SEAM at the WAISTLINE, do it on one side of the DART as shown.

4.
- This image shows the crossmark on the other side of the DART, at the PRINCESS SEAM.

5.
- The excess fabric is creased at the PRINCESS SEAM crossmark and folded toward the CF.
- Taper the dart to nothing toward the BUST APEX.
- Pin the dart down to the muslin as shown.

6.
- Smooth the muslin past the side seam.
- Pin the entire side seam.
- Smooth the fabric up and over the dress form ARMPLATE to the SHOULDER.
- Create a ¼" pinch (excess) at the SCREW LEVEL of the ARMHOLE. This makes sure the ARMHOLE isn't too tight.
- Leave all excess fabric in the SHOULDER AREA.
- Drape the FRONT NECKLINE.
- Trim and clip the neckline.

7.
- Drape the PRINCESS SHOULDER DART, folding toward the CF. Taper this dart toward the BUST APEX.
- Trim any excess fabric up to about 1 ½"-2" away from WAIST, SHOULDER, SIDE SEAM
- Mark all the key areas of the DRESS FORM to the fabric/muslin:
- NECKLINE: Crossmark at CF NECK and at NECKLINE/SHOULDER corner. Lightly mark the neckline.
- SHOULDER SEAM and SHOULDER DART: Mark SHOULDER seam and crossmark shoulder dart
- ARMPLATE: Crossmark at shoulder seam ridge (top of shoulder corner); middle of screw level; bottom of armplate at side seam.
- Mark the SIDE SEAM, WAIST, NECK, SHOULDER and middle of ARMHOLE.

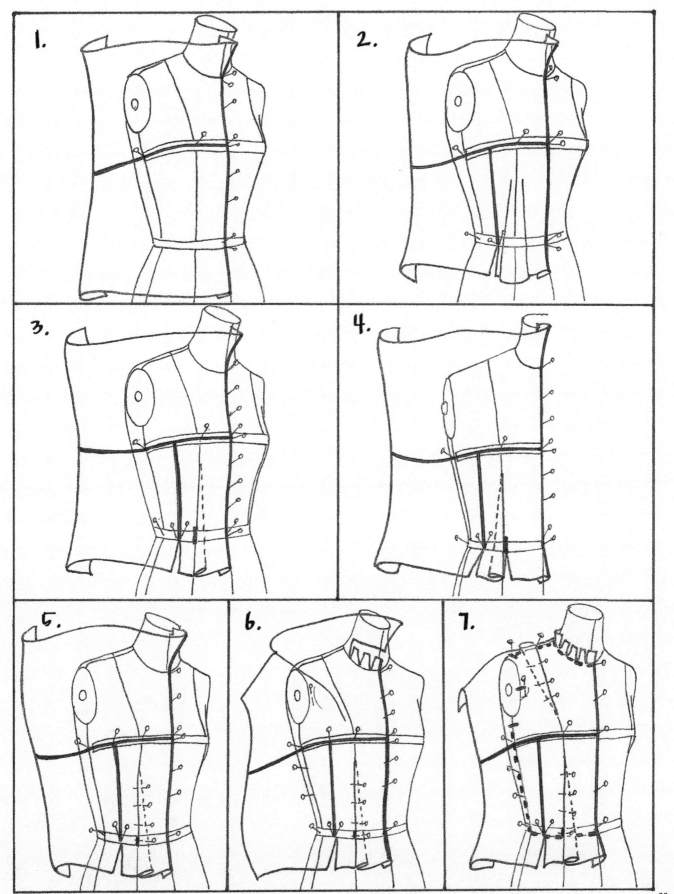

Basic Bodice

2 DART: FRONT & BACK

BACK DRAPE:
1) Take Back Prepped Muslin 25"L x 15" W Piece that has been folded under at CB.
2) Mark 3" from top edge at CB, write "Neckline".
3) From 3" mark, measure 4 ¼" down, mark, then draw a straight horizontal line across the muslin piece. This line represents the "Across Back" line
4) Measure CB to Armplate at this "Across Back" line, mark.

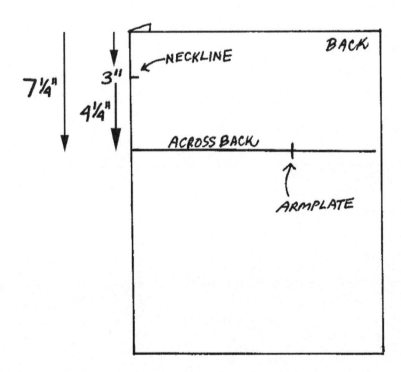

Now you can Drape the Back Bodice!

Basic Bodice

2 DART: BACK

1.
- Pin the CB GRAINLINE fold of the fabric to the CB position on the dress form.
- Align the NECKLINE POSITION MARK of the fabric to the CB neck position on the dress form.
- Pin and drape the BACK CROSSGRAIN LINE of the fabric to the shoulder blade level on the dress form.
- Pin the ARMPLATE CROSSMARK $\frac{1}{4}$" away from the armplate. Distribute the excess ease carefully and evenly.

2.
- Pin and drape the BACK WAIST DART—7" long by 1 $\frac{1}{4}$" wide (as shown) using the following steps:
  - Smooth the fabric toward the side seam and place a crossmark at the princess/waist seam (A).
  - Measure 1 $\frac{1}{4}$" toward the side seam and mark (B).
  - Then measure 7" up in the middle of the dart and mark; this will be the top end of the back waist dart.
  - Fold the back waist dart in place toward the CB and pin.

3.
- Clip and drape the WAISTLINE, smoothing toward the SIDE SEAM.
- Pin at the side seam/waist corner.
- Drape fabric beyond the SIDE SEAM and pin the SIDE SEAM.

4.
- Clip, smooth, and drape the BACK NECKLINE.
- Trim excess fabric around the neck area, clipping as you trim away.
- After you clip and trim the neckline, smooth fabric over the SHOULDER of the dress form and pin.

5.
- Drape the BACK SHOULDER DART, 3" long by $\frac{1}{2}$" wide.
- Smooth fabric over the shoulder seam, starting at the neckline and draping over the princess seam, crossmark.
- Measure toward the armhole $\frac{1}{2}$" from the princess seam at the shoulder, crossmark.
- Measure down 3" on the princess seam from the shoulder seam, crossmark.
- Fold the back shoulder dart in place, folding toward the CB, and pin.

6.
- Mark all the key area of the dress form to the fabric:
  - NECKLINE: crossmark at CB neck and at neckline/shoulder corner. Mark the rest of the neckline.
  - SHOULDER SEAM, SHOULDER DART: Mark the shoulder seam and crossmark the shoulder dart and shoulder edge/ridge.
  - ARMPLATE: Mark the top at shoulder edge/ridge. Mark middle at screw level. Mark the bottom of armplate at the side seam.
  - SIDE SEAM: Mark the side seam.
  - WAISTLINE and WAIST DART: Crossmark CB waist, side seam waist, both sides of the waist dart, and the rest of the waistline.

13.

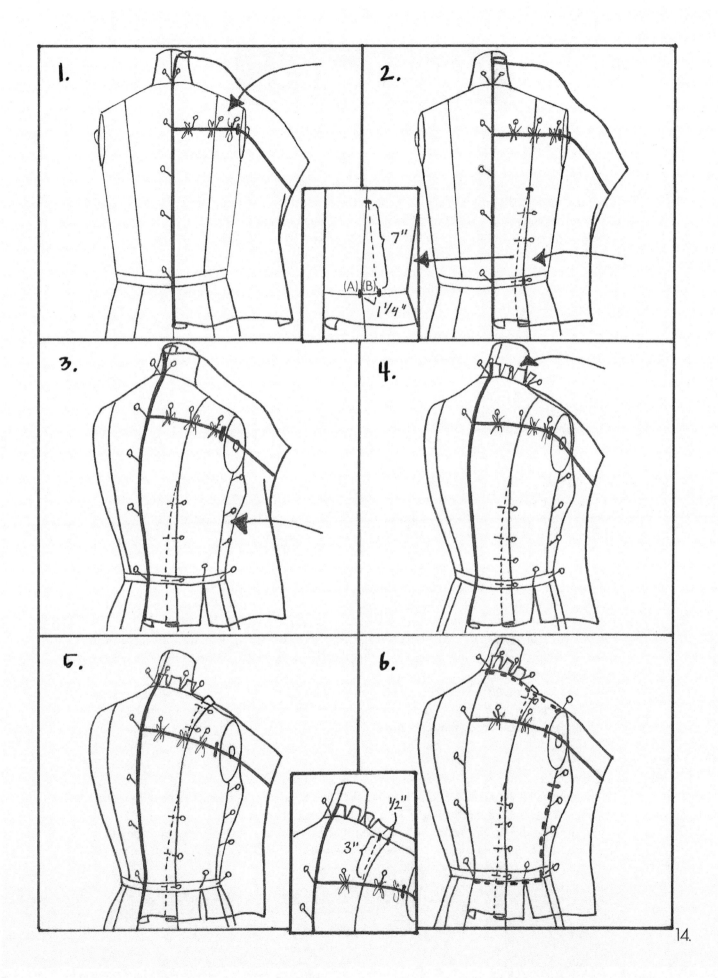

1.

2.

7"

(A) (B)

1¼"

3.

4.

5.

6.

½"

3"

14.

Basic Bodice

TRUEING THE DRAPE

1. Remove the fabric from the DRESS FORM and lay it flat on the pattern table.
- Cut pattern/dotted paper slightly larger than the draped muslin pieces.
- Draw a STRAIGHT OF GRAIN and CROSSGRAIN lines on the pattern paper.
- Place fabric on top of the paper matching the STRAIGHT and CROSSGRAIN lines.
- Transfer all the fabric markings, including crossmarks using a TRACING WHEEL.
- (OPTIONAL): If you want, after you have transferred the markings, lightly go over your transfered markings on the pattern paper with a pencil, to make sure you can see the markings.

2. Draw a SHORT 90 DEGREE angle LINE at:
- CF NECK: draw a $\frac{1}{4}$" line
- CF WAIST: draw a $\frac{1}{2}$" line
- CB NECK: draw a 1" line
- CB WAIST: draw a 1" line

3. Draw the 4 DARTS using a straight ruler:
- FRONT WAIST DART: Draw temporary "dart leg" lines from WAISTLINE crossmarks to the APEX mark. Draw additional dart leg lines INSIDE those outer dart leg lines starting 1" from the APEX. The inner dart leg lines will now be your actual FRONT WAIST DART.
- FRONT SHOULDER DART: Draw the dart legs from the SHOULDER crossmarks to the APEX. Then, staring 1" away from the APEX, draw INNER dart leg lines, to the SHOULDER crossmarks. The inner dart leg lines will now be your actual FRONT SHOULDER DART.
- BACK DARTS: First, from the WAIST dart crossmark, closest to the BACK, draw a STRAIGHT LINE that goes all the way up to the SHOULDER dart crossmark, closest to CB NECK.
- BACK WAIST DART: Draw a crossmark on the STRAIGHT LINE 7" up from the crossmark at the waist "A". Then, from the other crossmark at the WAIST, draw a staight line to the 7" mark creating your back waist dart.
- BACK SHOULDER DART: Draw a crossmark on the STRAIGHT LINE 3" down from the crossmark at the shoulder "B". Then, from the other crossmark at the SHOULDER, draw a staight line to the 3" mark creating your back shoulder dart.

4. Draw the FRONT and BACK NECKLINES using the French Curve:
- Draw the FRONT and BACK necklines, using the French Curve, as shown. Connect your short 90 degree line you created in Step 2 with the neck crossmark.
- When drawing the curve, make sure to blend the lines smoothly into the 90 degree angles at the CF and CB necklines, making sure that the lines DO NOT COME TO A POINT.

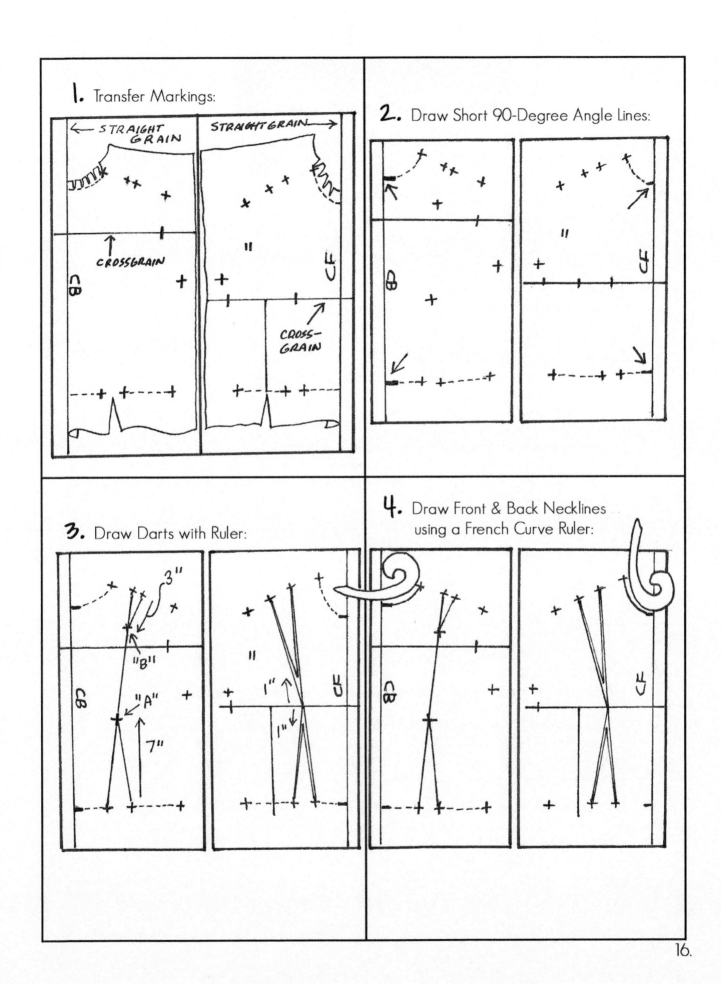

1. Transfer Markings:

2. Draw Short 90-Degree Angle Lines:

3. Draw Darts with Ruler:

4. Draw Front & Back Necklines using a French Curve Ruler:

16.

TRUEING THE DRAPE

5. Draw the FRONT and BACK SHOULDER SEAMS:
- Fold the SHOULDER DARTS into position on the dotted pattern paper; notice the direction of the fold in the images, the folds are toward the CFront and the CBack, respectively.
- In order to hold the folds down, you might want to pin them down.
- Once you have done this, using a straight ruler, draw a STRAIGHT line at the SHOULDER, from the shoulder neck corner to the shoulder edge corner.

6. Draw the FRONT and BACK WAISTLINE:
- Fold the WAISTLINE DARTS closed, on the dotted pattern paper.
- Notice the direction of the fold in the images: For the FRONT WAISTLINE DART, fold toward the FRONT and for the BACK WAISTLINE DART, fold toward the BACK. You can pin the folded darts down to help hold them down.
- Using the hip curve ruler, for the FRONT draw the waistline smoothly from the CFront to the side seam. And then for the BACK, blend/draw the waistline smoothly from CBack to the side seam. Notice the position of the hip curve ruler: curved part is toward the side seam and straight part is toward CF and CB.

7. Draw temporary SIDE SEAMS:
- Using a straight ruler, connect the crossmark at the ARMPLATE/SIDE SEAM to the crossmark at the WAIST/SIDE SEAM for both the FRONT and BACK.
- This line will be "temporary" and only serve as a guide to draw the actual side seam with ease (next step).

8. Add SIDE SEAM ease:
- At the UNDERARM/SIDE SEAM, crossmark 1" down from the armplate/side seam crossmarks.
- From this point, add ½" to the SIDE SEAM line, this will be body ease.
- Connect the 1" crossmark with the ½" crossmark with a short straight horizontal line.
- Then, draw a straight line from this new armhole/underarm point to the waist/side seam. This line will now be your new SIDE SEAM.

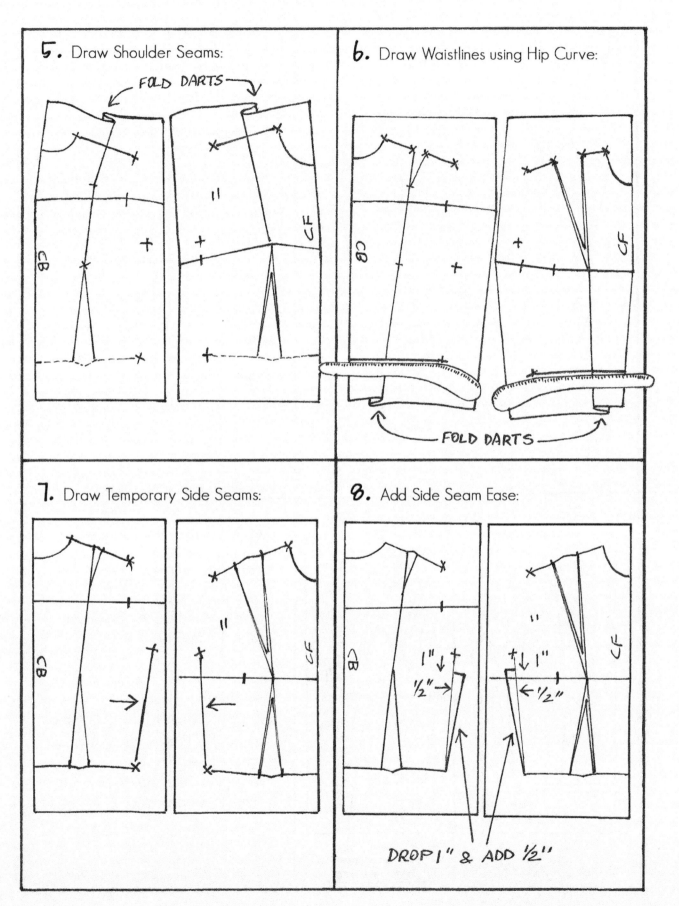

5. Draw Shoulder Seams:

FOLD DARTS

CB

CF

6. Draw Waistlines using Hip Curve:

CB

CF

FOLD DARTS

7. Draw Temporary Side Seams:

CB

CF

8. Add Side Seam Ease:

CB

CF

1"↓

½"→

↓1"

←½"

DROP 1" & ADD ½"

9. Check The Waistline Curve:

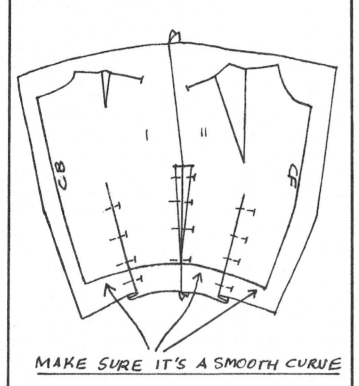

MAKE SURE IT'S A SMOOTH CURVE

- Pin the trued SIDE SEAMS together on the pattern/dotted paper as shown.
- The waistline should be drawn in one continuous line.
- Sometimes a slight readjustment is needed if the side seams for the FRONT and BACK, respectively, are not the same length (this can happen because of inaccurate draping and is common).
- Make sure both side seams are THE SAME length. If not, split the Difference: Add to the front and take out from the back, or visa versa.
- Once you have done this, then you can draw in the proper waistline.

10. Draw The Armholes Using The French Curve:

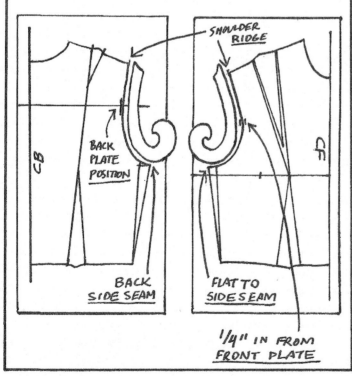

SHOULDER RIDGE

CB

BACK PLATE POSITION

BACK SIDE SEAM

FLAT TO SIDE SEAM

CF

1/4" IN FROM FRONT PLATE

USING THE FRENCH CURVE:

- BACK: Connect the following positions:
  - o Back SHOULDER RIDGE corner
  - o Back PLATE position
  - o New SIDE SEAM position, at the 1" drop position

- FRONT: Connect the following positions:
  - o Front SHOULDER RIDGE corner
  - o Front PLATE position ¼" from the plate towards CF
  - o Original SIDE SEAM position, at the 1" drop position

BASIC BODICE

ADDING SEAM ALLOWANCE TO MUSLIN DRAPE

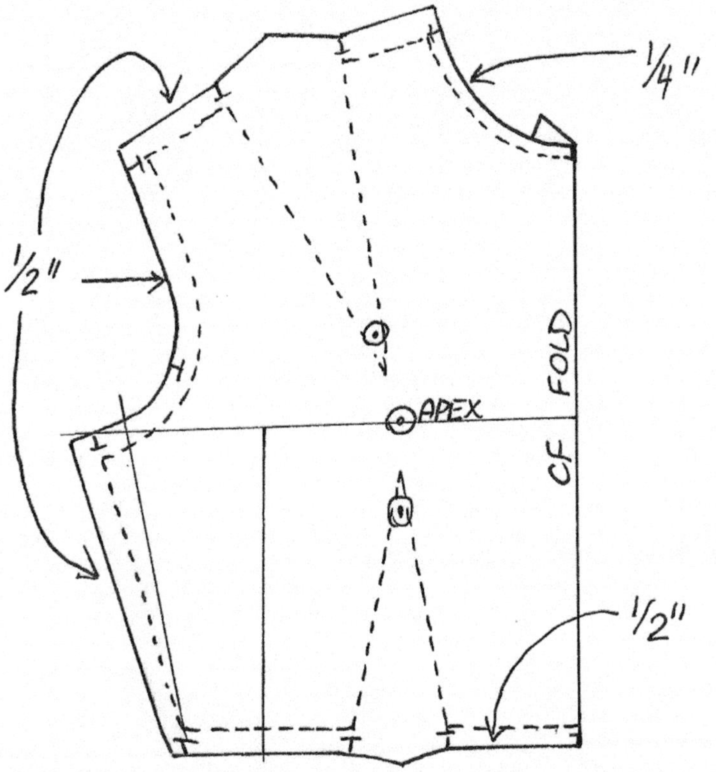

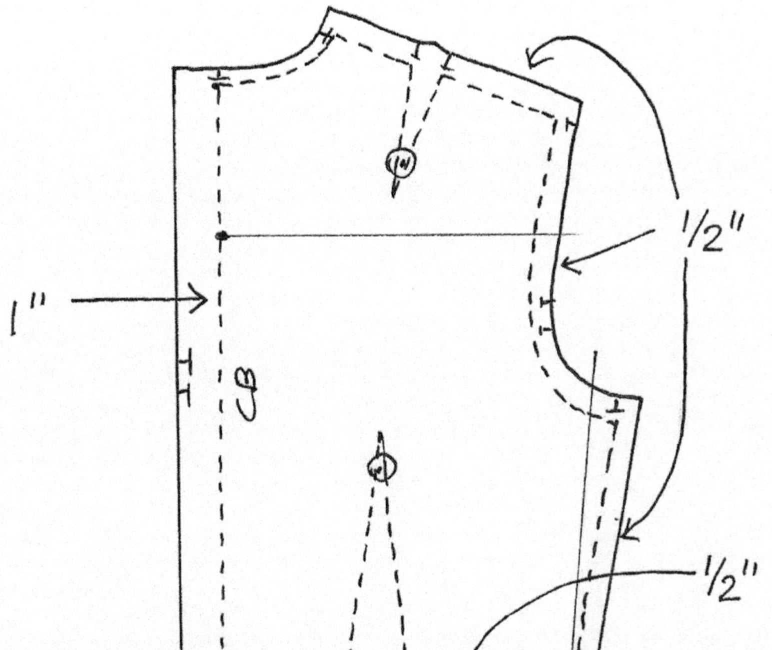

BASIC SLEEVE

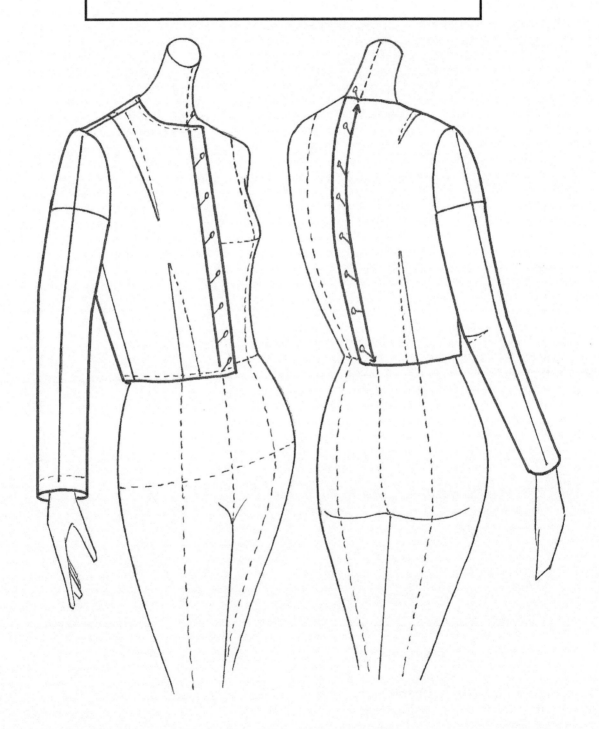

BASIC SLEEVE

In order to draft the Basic Sleeve, study these FIVE important MEASUREMENTS:

1. OVERARM LENGTH: Distance from the shoulder to the wrist

Dress Form Size	Measurement
6	22 3/8" (56.8 cm)
8	22 ¾" (57.8 cm)
10	23 1/8" (58.7 cm)
12	23 ½" (59.7 cm)

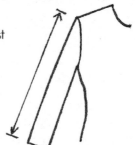

2. UNDERARM LENGTH: Distance from the underarm to the wrist

Dress Form Size	Measurement
6	6 ¼" (41.3 cm)
8	16 ½" (41.9 cm)
10	16 ¾" (42.5 cm)
12	17" (43.2 cm)

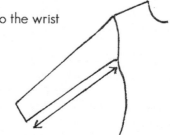

3. CAP HEIGHT: Distance from the underarm armpit to the shoulder

Dress Form Size	Measurement
6	6 1/8" (15.6 cm)
8	6 ¼" (15.9 cm)
10	6 3/8" (16.2 cm)
12	6 ½" (16.5 cm)

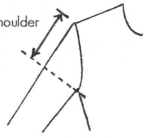

4. ELBOW CIRCUMFERENCE: Measurement around the elbow plus 1" for ease

Dress Form Size	Measurement
6	9 ¾" (24.8 cm)
8	10 ¼" (26.0 cm)
10	10 ¾" (27.3 cm)
12	11 ¼" (28.6 cm)

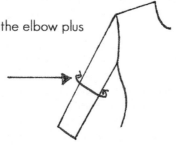

5. BICEP CIRCUMFERENCE: Measurement around upper arm plus 2" ease

Dress Form Size	Measurement
6	11 ½" (29.2 cm)
8	12" (30.5 cm)
10	12 ½" (31.8 cm)
12	13" (33.0 cm)

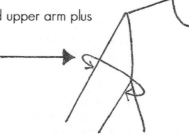

Knit Sleeve

In order to draft the BASIC KNIT SLEEVE, study these 4 important MEASUREMENT GUIDES:

1. OVERALL LENGTH: Distance from the shoulder to the wrist

SIZE	MEASUREMENT
6	22 1/2" (57.2 cm)
8	22 3/4" (57.8 cm)
10	23" (58.4 cm)
12	23 1/4" (59.7 cm)

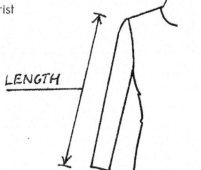

2. CAP HEIGHT: From armpit position to shoulder

SIZE	MEASUREMENT
6	5 1/8" (13 cm)
8	5 1/4" (13.3 cm)
10	5 3/8" (13.7 cm)
12	5 5/8" (14.3 cm)

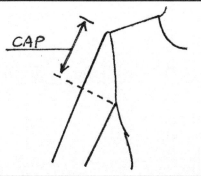

3. ELBOW CIRCUMFERENCE: Measure around the elbow plus 2" of ease

SIZE	MEASUREMENT--These are all HALF measurements
6	4 1/8" (10.5 cm)
8	4 1/4" (10.8 cm)
10	4 3/8" (11.1 cm)
12	4 5.8" (11.8 cm)

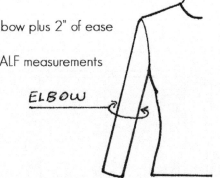

4. BICEP CIRCUMFERENCE: Measure around the upper arm plus 2" of ease

SIZE	MEASUREMENT
6	5 1/8" (13 cm)
8	5 1/4" (13.3 cm)
10	5 3/8" (13.7 cm)
12	5 5/8" (14.3 cm)

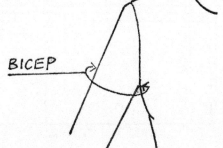

BASIC SLEEVE
HOW TO DRAFT

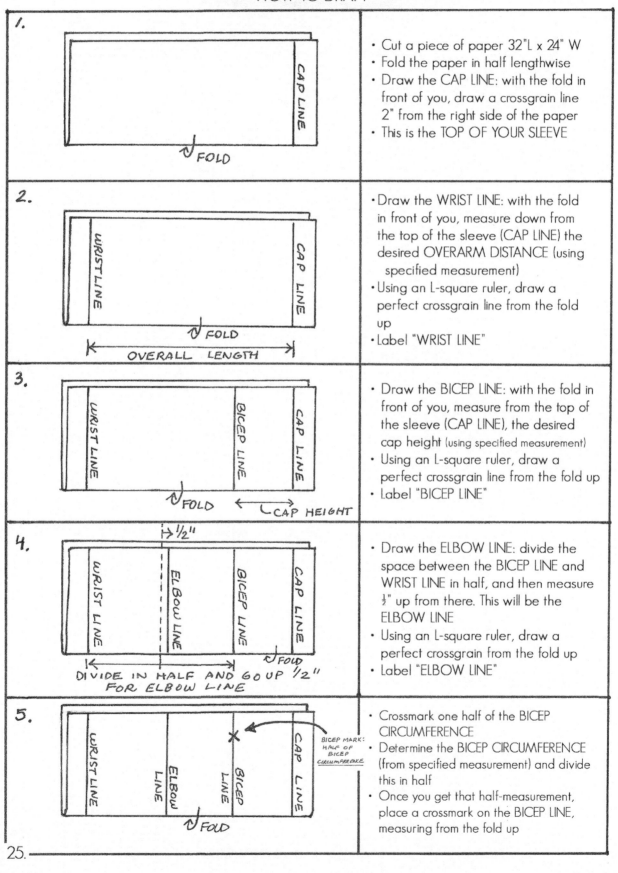

1.
- Cut a piece of paper 32"L x 24" W
- Fold the paper in half lengthwise
- Draw the CAP LINE: with the fold in front of you, draw a crossgrain line 2" from the right side of the paper
- This is the TOP OF YOUR SLEEVE

2.
- Draw the WRIST LINE: with the fold in front of you, measure down from the top of the sleeve (CAP LINE) the desired OVERARM DISTANCE (using specified measurement)
- Using an L-square ruler, draw a perfect crossgrain line from the fold up
- Label "WRIST LINE"

3.
- Draw the BICEP LINE: with the fold in front of you, measure from the top of the sleeve (CAP LINE), the desired cap height (using specified measurement)
- Using an L-square ruler, draw a perfect crossgrain line from the fold up
- Label "BICEP LINE"

4.
- Draw the ELBOW LINE: divide the space between the BICEP LINE and WRIST LINE in half, and then measure ½" up from there. This will be the ELBOW LINE
- Using an L-square ruler, draw a perfect crossgrain from the fold up
- Label "ELBOW LINE"

5.
- Crossmark one half of the BICEP CIRCUMFERENCE
- Determine the BICEP CIRCUMFERENCE (from specified measurement) and divide this in half
- Once you get that half-measurement, place a crossmark on the BICEP LINE, measuring from the fold up

25.

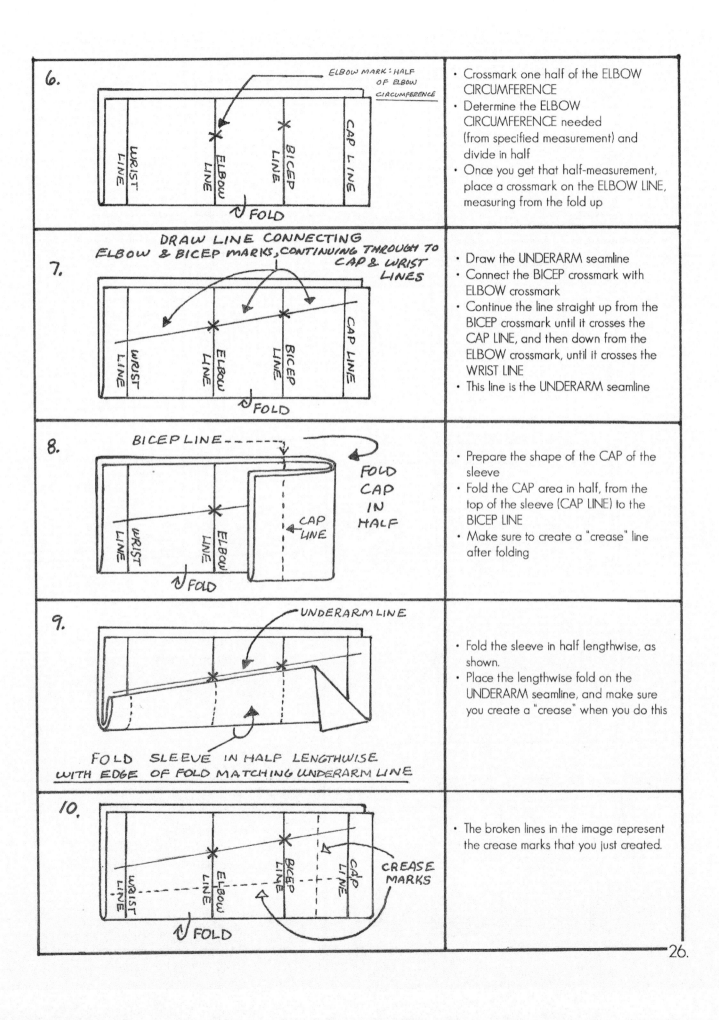

6.

ELBOW MARK : HALF OF ELBOW CIRCUMFERENCE

WRIST LINE
ELBOW LINE
BICEP LINE
CAP LINE

FOLD

- Crossmark one half of the ELBOW CIRCUMFERENCE
- Determine the ELBOW CIRCUMFERENCE needed (from specified measurement) and divide in half
- Once you get that half-measurement, place a crossmark on the ELBOW LINE, measuring from the fold up

7.

DRAW LINE CONNECTING ELBOW & BICEP MARKS, CONTINUING THROUGH TO CAP & WRIST LINES

WRIST LINE
ELBOW LINE
BICEP LINE
CAP LINE

FOLD

- Draw the UNDERARM seamline
- Connect the BICEP crossmark with ELBOW crossmark
- Continue the line straight up from the BICEP crossmark until it crosses the CAP LINE, and then down from the ELBOW crossmark, until it crosses the WRIST LINE
- This line is the UNDERARM seamline

8.

BICEP LINE

FOLD CAP IN HALF

WRIST LINE
ELBOW LINE
CAP LINE

FOLD

- Prepare the shape of the CAP of the sleeve
- Fold the CAP area in half, from the top of the sleeve (CAP LINE) to the BICEP LINE
- Make sure to create a "crease" line after folding

9.

UNDERARM LINE

FOLD SLEEVE IN HALF LENGTHWISE WITH EDGE OF FOLD MATCHING UNDERARM LINE

- Fold the sleeve in half lengthwise, as shown.
- Place the lengthwise fold on the UNDERARM seamline, and make sure you create a "crease" when you do this

10.

WRIST LINE
ELBOW LINE
BICEP LINE
CAP LINE

CREASE MARKS

FOLD

- The broken lines in the image represent the crease marks that you just created.

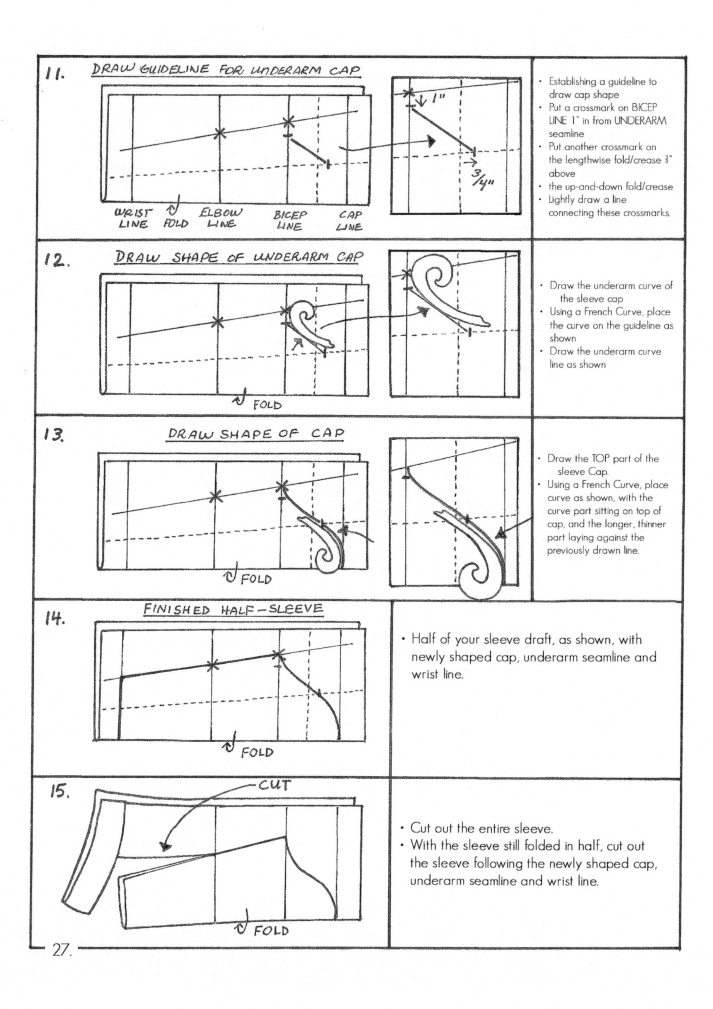

11. <u>DRAW GUIDELINE FOR UNDERARM CAP</u>

↓ 1"

3/4"

WRIST LINE   ↲ FOLD   ELBOW LINE   BICEP LINE   CAP LINE

- Establishing a guideline to draw cap shape
- Put a crossmark on BICEP LINE 1" in from UNDERARM seamline
- Put another crossmark on the lengthwise fold/crease 3/4" above
- the up-and-down fold/crease
- Lightly draw a line connecting these crossmarks.

12. <u>DRAW SHAPE OF UNDERARM CAP</u>

↲ FOLD

- Draw the underarm curve of the sleeve cap
- Using a French Curve, place the curve on the guideline as shown
- Draw the underarm curve line as shown

13. <u>DRAW SHAPE OF CAP</u>

↲ FOLD

- Draw the TOP part of the sleeve Cap.
- Using a French Curve, place curve as shown, with the curve part sitting on top of cap, and the longer, thinner part laying against the previously drawn line.

14. <u>FINISHED HALF-SLEEVE</u>

↲ FOLD

- Half of your sleeve draft, as shown, with newly shaped cap, underarm seamline and wrist line.

15. CUT

↲ FOLD

- Cut out the entire sleeve.
- With the sleeve still folded in half, cut out the sleeve following the newly shaped cap, underarm seamline and wrist line.

27.

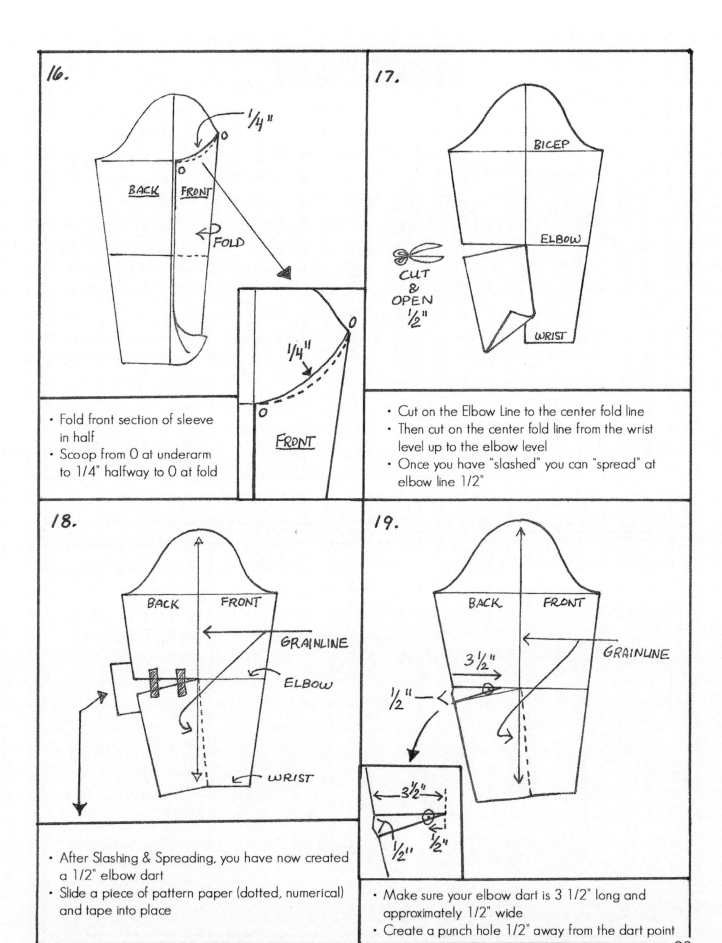

16.

1/4"

O

O

BACK   FRONT

FOLD

1/4"

O

O

FRONT

- Fold front section of sleeve in half
- Scoop from 0 at underarm to 1/4" halfway to 0 at fold

17.

BICEP

ELBOW

CUT & OPEN 1/2"

WRIST

- Cut on the Elbow Line to the center fold line
- Then cut on the center fold line from the wrist level up to the elbow level
- Once you have "slashed" you can "spread" at elbow line 1/2"

18.

BACK   FRONT

GRAINLINE

ELBOW

WRIST

- After Slashing & Spreading, you have now created a 1/2" elbow dart
- Slide a piece of pattern paper (dotted, numerical) and tape into place

19.

BACK   FRONT

GRAINLINE

3 1/2"

1/2"

3 1/2"

1/2"   1/2"

- Make sure your elbow dart is 3 1/2" long and approximately 1/2" wide
- Create a punch hole 1/2" away from the dart point

20.

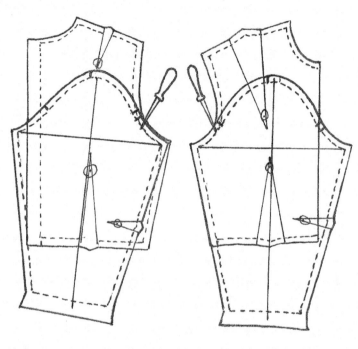

- In order to make sure that your sleeve fits properly whenever there is a sleeve in a garment, it is essential that one "walks the sleeve" to the armhole.

- "Walking The Sleeve" ensures that notches match and that there is the right amount of cap ease so the sleeve does not fit to snuggly around the cap (top) of the sleeve.

- "Walking The Sleeve" will also ensure that the sleeve can be sewn correctly to the bodice.

- Normally, you want approximately 1"-1¼" of extra ease when walking the sleeve to the armhole. In other words, the total measurement of the sleeve cap should be 1"-1 ¼" longer than the total armhole measurement.

21.

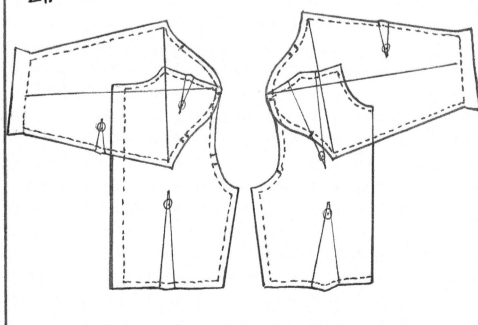

- When walking the sleeve to the armhole, using an awl, begin at the underarm and begin walking the sleeve pattern slowly, moving it in ¼" intervals.

- Think of it as if you were sewing the sleeve to the armhole but very, very slowly.

- When walking the sleeve pattern to the armhole, match the front and back notches in the armhole, and then continue walking up to the cap.

22.

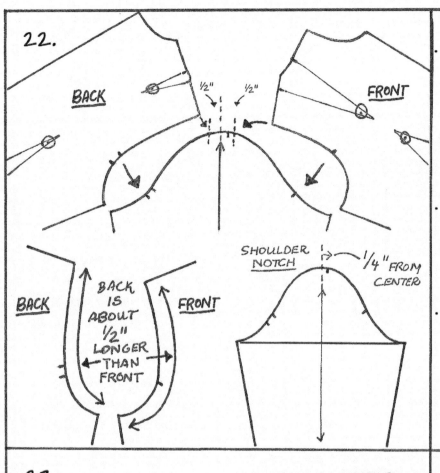

BACK

FRONT

½"   ½"

SHOULDER NOTCH   ¼" FROM CENTER

BACK

BACK IS ABOUT ½" LONGER THAN FRONT

FRONT

- If you walked the pattern correctly, the shoulder of your back bodice pattern should end about ½" away from the center of the sleeve, and the shoulder of your front bodice pattern should end about ½" away from the center of the sleeve.

- The shoulder notch of the sleeve should end up ¼" toward the front of the sleeve, as shown and NOT in the actual center of the cap of your sleeve.

- The Back Armhole measurement should be about ½"-¾" LONGER than the Front Armhole.

23.

SLASH & CLOSE

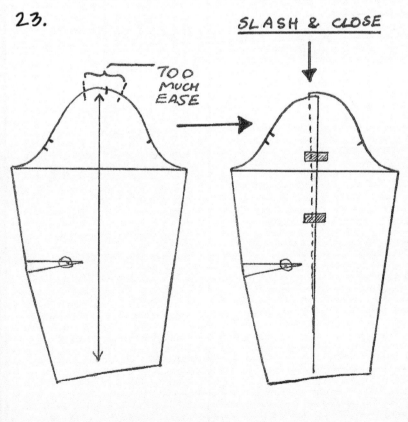

TOO MUCH EASE

If The Cap Ease is Too Much

Solution #1:
- Adjust the Sleeve Pattern but NOT the Armhole of the Bodice.

- Using the "Slash & Spread" Method to Slash & Remove.

- Cut sleeve pattern from the wrist to the cap in the center of the sleeve and decrease cap width as shown.

- Fold over one side of the sleeve until you have decreased amount of sleeve cap to your desired amount. Tape down.

- Redraw center grainline of the sleeve.

- Walk the sleeve to the bodice's armhole until it walks properly.

24.

A.

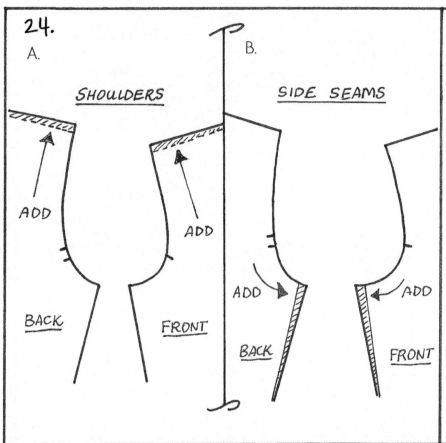

SHOULDERS

ADD

ADD

BACK   FRONT

B.

SIDE SEAMS

ADD

ADD

BACK   FRONT

If Cap Ease is Too Much
Solution #2:
• Leave the Sleeve pattern
  the same but adjust the
  armholes to add to their
  overall length, to make up
  for the extra ease in the
  sleeve.

• You can either:
   A. Add small amount to
      the shoulders at the
      armhole
   B. Add small amount to
      the side seams at the
      armhole

• Try walking the sleeve
  now to the armhole and
  see if the ease has been
  decreased.

25.

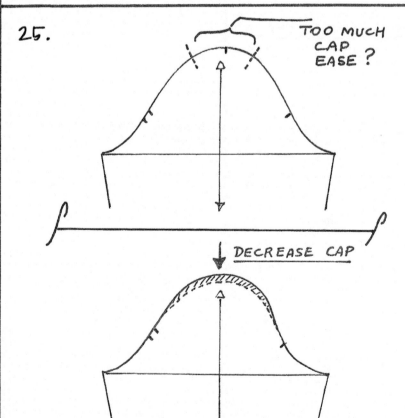

TOO MUCH
CAP
EASE ?

DECREASE CAP

If Cap Ease is Too Much

Solution #3:
• Leave the bodice armhole
  the same but adjust the
  cap of sleeve.
• Decrease cap height by
  1/8"- 1/4" and see if this
  helps decrease total cap
  ease.
• Walk newly adjusted
  sleeve to the armhole and
  check ease amount. Total
  ease should be 1"-1 $\frac{1}{2}$",
  anymore than this and you
  will get unnecessary
  gathering.

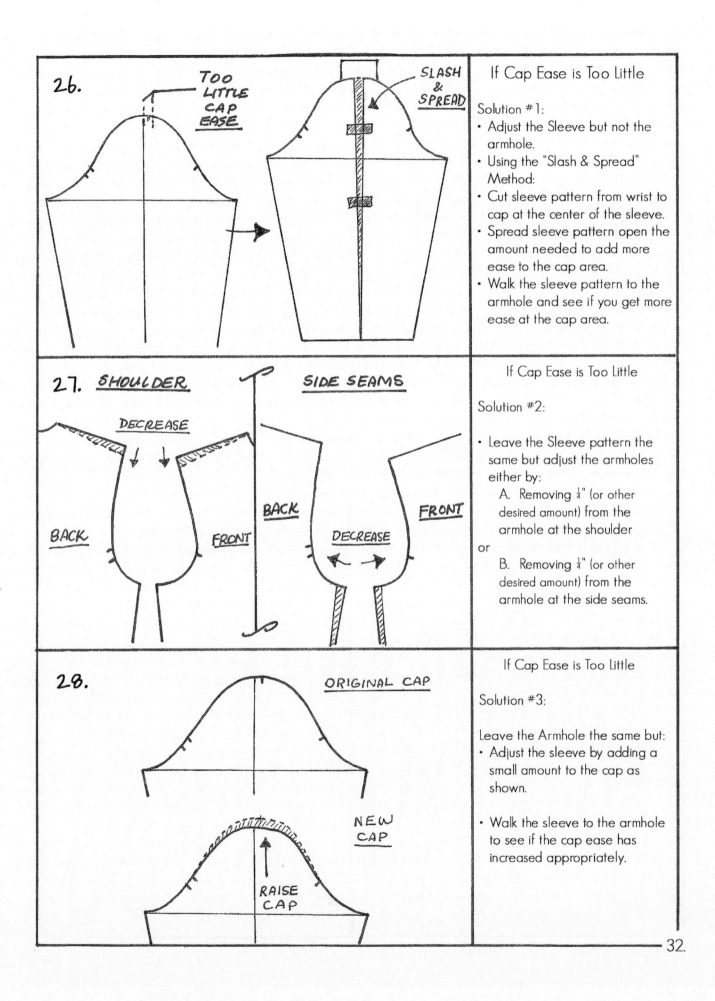

26.

TOO LITTLE CAP EASE

SLASH & SPREAD

If Cap Ease is Too Little

Solution #1:
- Adjust the Sleeve but not the armhole.
- Using the "Slash & Spread" Method:
- Cut sleeve pattern from wrist to cap at the center of the sleeve.
- Spread sleeve pattern open the amount needed to add more ease to the cap area.
- Walk the sleeve pattern to the armhole and see if you get more ease at the cap area.

27. SHOULDER

SIDE SEAMS

DECREASE

BACK

FRONT

BACK

FRONT

DECREASE

If Cap Ease is Too Little

Solution #2:

- Leave the Sleeve pattern the same but adjust the armholes either by:

    A. Removing $\frac{1}{4}$" (or other desired amount) from the armhole at the shoulder
or
    B. Removing $\frac{1}{4}$" (or other desired amount) from the armhole at the side seams.

28.

ORIGINAL CAP

NEW CAP

RAISE CAP

If Cap Ease is Too Little

Solution #3:

Leave the Armhole the same but:
- Adjust the sleeve by adding a small amount to the cap as shown.

- Walk the sleeve to the armhole to see if the cap ease has increased appropriately.

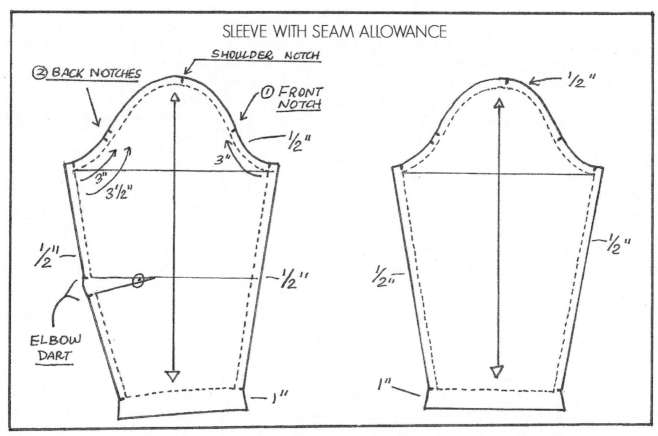

SLEEVE WITH SEAM ALLOWANCE

SHOULDER NOTCH

② BACK NOTCHES

① FRONT NOTCH

½"

3"

3"

3½"

½"

½"

ELBOW DART

1"

½"

½"

½"

1"

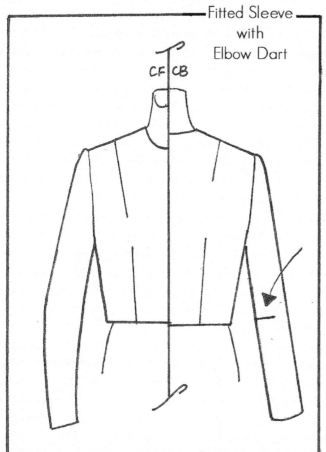

Fitted Sleeve
with
Elbow Dart

CF CB

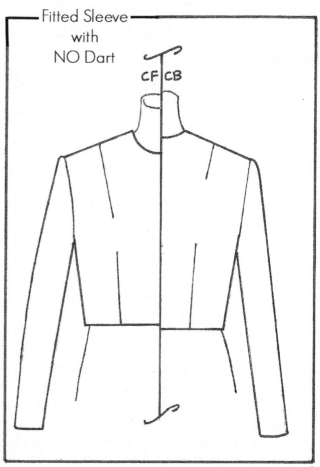

Fitted Sleeve
with
NO Dart

CF CB

33.

BASIC FITTED SKIRT

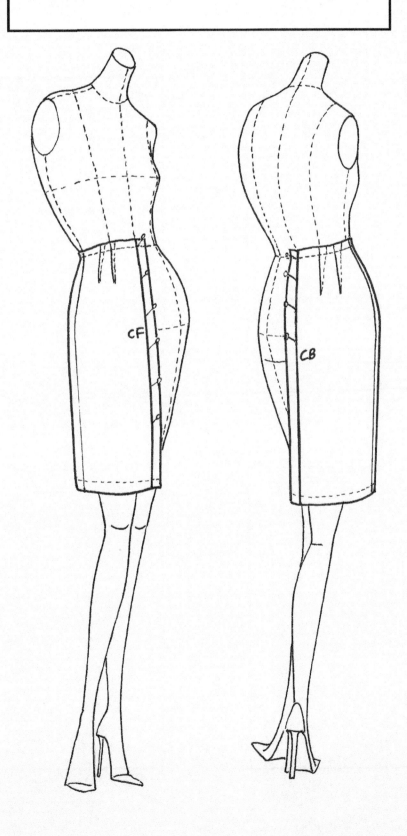

Basic Fitted Skirt

Preparing the Muslin for the Front and Back Skirt Drape:

- Cut 2 pieces of muslin 30" L x 20" W
- Mark grainlines CF and CB 1" away from edges/selvage
- Label each piece of muslin accordingly "Front" and "Back

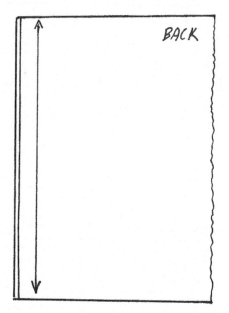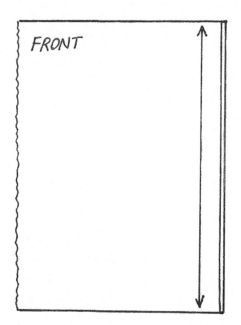

- Press under each of the 2 pieces of muslin at the 1" grainline:

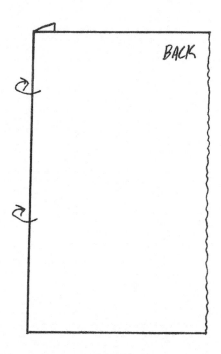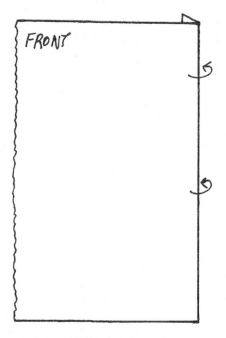

Preparing the Muslin for the Front and Back Skirt Drape:

1. For BOTH the FRONT and BACK SKIRT cut pieces:
   - On the folded CF edge, measure 3" down from the top and mark. This will be the CF WAIST. Repeat the above for the BACK SKIRT, from the folded CB edge.

2. From this mark, measure 7" down and mark. This is the HIPLINE. Repeat the above for the BACK SKIRT.

3. At the HIPLINE mark, draw a crossgrain line from the CF and CB folded edges. Use your L-square to make this line.

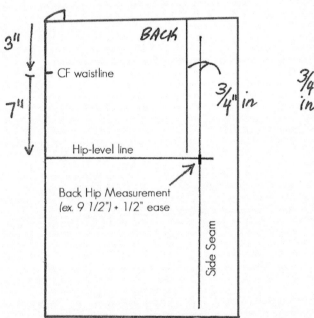
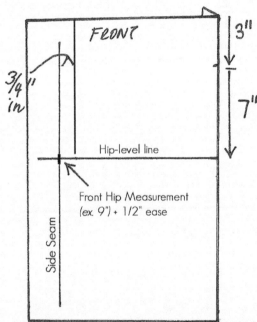

4. Determine the FRONT SIDE SEAM:
   - For the FRONT: measure the hip measurement on the dress form and add ½" for ease (for example, front hip measurement is 9", add ½" for ease, therefore total measurement = 9 ½")
   - Mark this measurement on the crossgrain and draw a straight up-and-down line that is parallel to the CF grainline/folded edge.

5. Determine the BACK SIDE SEAM:
   - For the BACK: measure the hip measurement on the dress form and add ½" for ease (for example, back hip measurement is 9 ½", add ½" for ease, therefore total measurement = 10")
   - Normally the BACK hip measurement is ½" longer than the FRONT
   - Mark this measurement on the crossgrain and draw a straight up-and-down line that is parallel to the CB grainline/folded edge.

6. Draw a secondary side seam line on BOTH the FRONT and BACK SKIRT. This line will go from the top edge to slightly past the HIPLINE, as shown.
   - Measure ¾" toward the CF/CB from the SIDE SEAM line on both the FRONT and BACK SKIRT. This line will be used to help drape in the WAISTLINE.

Basic Fitted Skirt

2 DART: FRONT

1.
- Pin the CF grainline fold of the fabric on the CF position of the dress form.
- When pinning, make sure to match the CROSSGRAIN/hip line of the fabric to the hip line of the dress form.

2.
- Smooth and pin the crossgrain line of the fabric (at the hip level), evenly distributing the ease (about ½" extra ease) across the dress form to the side seam, making sure the side seam line lands on the side seam of the dress form.
- This crossgrain/hip line should be parallel/horizontal to the floor and not askew.
- Pin the side seam, from hip level (approximately 7" below waist) to the bottom of the dress form.

3.
- Pin the front ¾" line (the shorter line) to the waist/side seam corner.
- After pinning, you will see slight excess fabric between the side seam and CF in the waist area. This excess will be draped into two small waist darts.

4.
- Drape the two small waist darts.
    - *(Optional: You can "pre-drape" your darts by folding two darts at the waist area, one at the princess seam and one between the princess seam and side seam. When folding them, try to get them to be the same width).*
- Smooth your fabric from CF to the princess seam and draw a crossmark at the princess seam. From that crossmark, take about ½" (could be slightly less or more) of fabric and fold into a dart and pin. This becomes your first waist dart.
- Crossmark the other end of that fold so when you open the dart/fold up, you know how wide it is.
- Now, measure 1 ¼" from the princess seam and crossmark. Take the remainder of the excess fabric and repeat the same steps you did for draping the first dart.
- Pin and crossmark the other end of the fold/dart, repeating the same steps you did for the first dart.
- If you evenly folded each dart, the rest of your waist, from that dart to the side seam, should be smooth with no excess fabric.
- Each dart will be about 3 ½" long but that is done when you true the skirt drape afterward.
- Smooth and drape the hips, and pin.
- Finish by marking the waist, hips (by lightly rubbing the hip area with your pencil)
- Keep FRONT skirt drape pinned on the dress form.

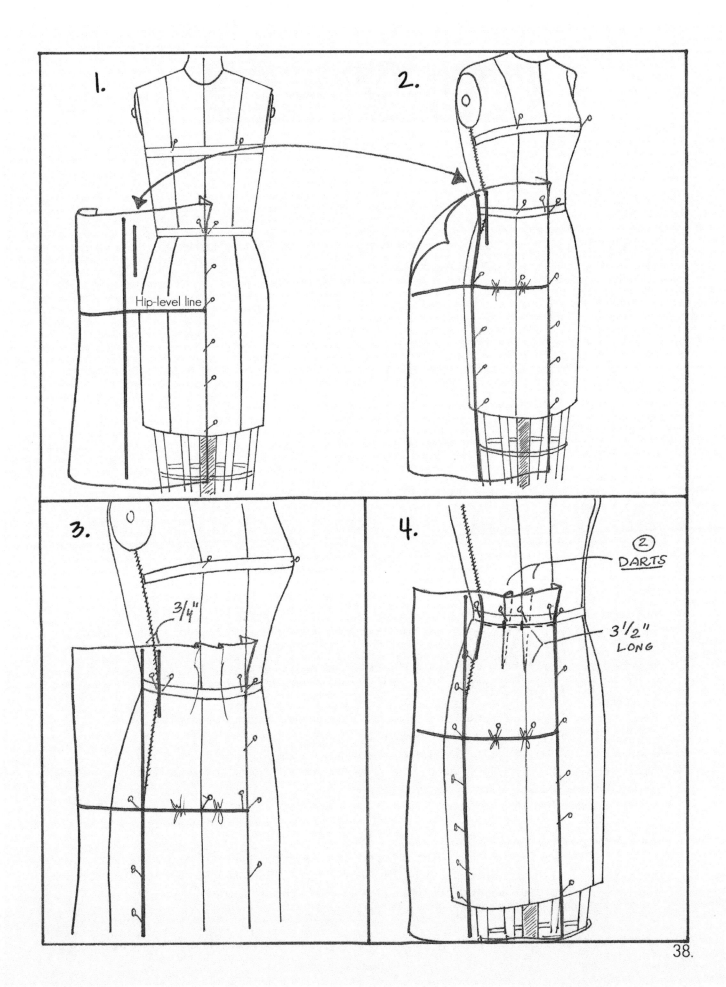

1.

Hip-level line

2.

3.

3/4"

4.

② DARTS

3 1/2" LONG

38.

Basic Fitted Skirt

2 DART: BACK

1.
- Pin the CB fold of your prepared fabric onto the CB of the dress form.
- When pinning the back, make sure to match the crossgrain line of the fabric to the hipline of the dress form, in the same manner you did for the front skirt drape.
- Pin the crossgrain line on the hip of the dress form, distributing the ease (about $\frac{1}{2}$") evenly, until you end up at the side seam.

2.
- Smooth the skirt to the side seam so the side seam line ends on the side seam of the dress form. Drape over the front skirt at the side as shown.
- To make things easier, you can remove the pins on the side seam (from your previous front skirt drape), to then pin the back skirt at the side seam onto the dress form.

3.
- Pin the $\frac{3}{4}$" line (smaller line) at the waist/side seam position of the dress form, draping it over the front skirt drape, as shown.
- When you do this, you will notice excess fabric created between CB at side seam at the waist area. These will become the back waist darts.

4.
- Drape the back waist darts.
  - *(Optional: You can "pre-drape" your darts by folding two darts at the waist area, one at the princess seam and one between the princess seam and side seam. When folding them, try to get them to be the same width).*
- Begin by draping the first back waist dart on the princess seam.
- Smooth the fabric from CB to princess seam and crossmark at the waist/princess seam. This will be one "end" of your dart.
- Measure about 1" (could be slightly less or more) and draw another crossmark. This will be the other "end" of your dart. Now, fold the dart and pin at the waist.
- Measure 1 $\frac{1}{4}$" from that first dart at the waist and crossmark.
- Measure about 1" (could be slightly less or more) to then create your second back waist dart. Crossmark. Fold the dart and pin. Now you have your second back waist dart.
- Both of these folds (that created the two back darts) should be even in width.
- Once you have evenly distributed your excess fabric into those two back darts, then the rest of your back skirt drape should be smooth, with no excess fabric.
- Pin the rest of the skirt from the second dart, to the side seam/waist position.
- The length of each back dart will be 5 $\frac{1}{2}$" long. This measurement will be done when you true the skirt drape.
- Finish by marking the waist, hips (by lightly rubbing the hip area with your pencil).

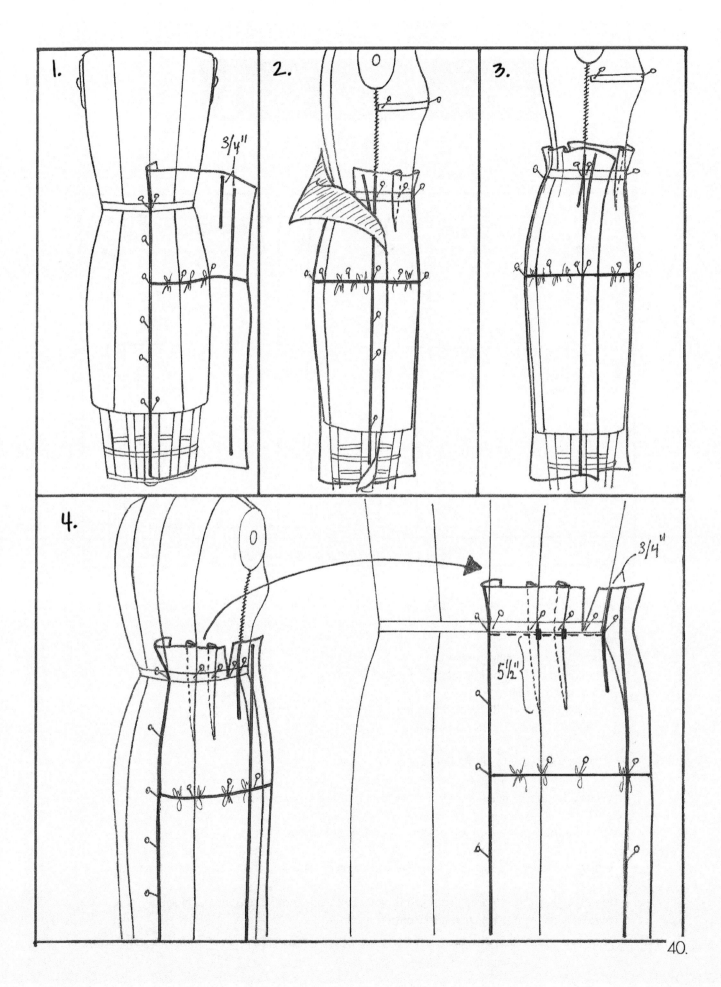

1.

3/4"

2.

3.

4.

3/4"

5½"

Basic Fitted Skirt

TRUEING THE SKIRT DRAPES

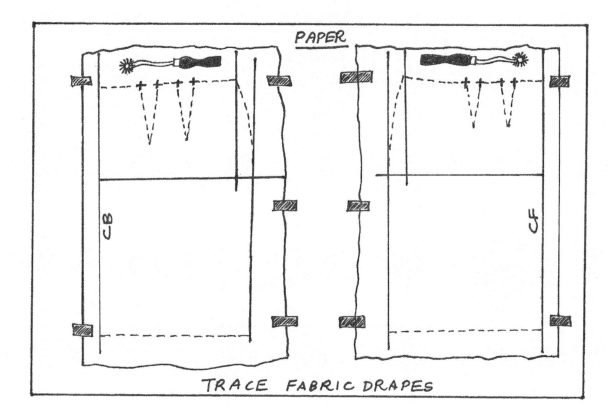

TRACE FABRIC DRAPES

Once you are done draping the Basic Skirt-Front and Back, it is time to TRUE the drape. Trueing is the process of correcting the drape. The steps in making your drape "true" involve the following:

- smoothing lines and curves
- squaring off the corners (hems, CF and CB waists)
- straightening lines
- making the darts the proper lengths
- balancing the draped patterns

Follow the steps below to TRUE your drape:

- Remove the fabric/muslin from the dress form and lay it flat on the pattern table.

- Place the fabric drape on top of the dotted pattern paper.

- To help in holding the fabric drape, you can carefully tape it to the dotted pattern paper.

- Using the TRACING WHEEL, transfer the waistline, darts, side seams, hem, hip-line, as well as any remaining crossmarks onto the paper.

41.

Basic Fitted Skirt

TRUEING THE SKIRT DRAPES

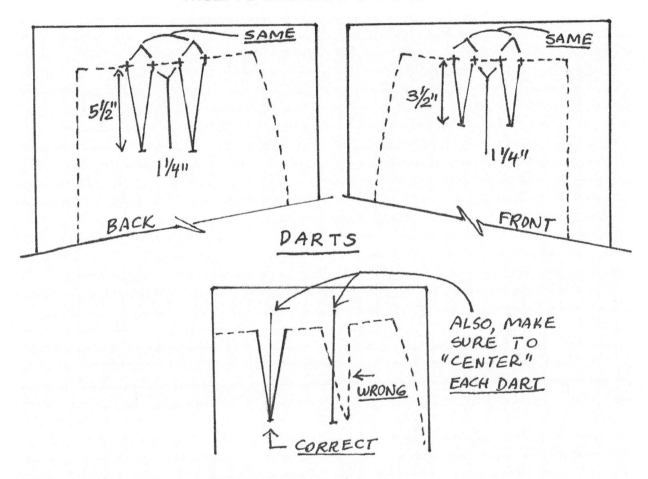

FOR THE DARTS:

FRONT:
- Measure the width of each dart and make sure they are the same. If not, equalize them *EX: if one is 1" and the other 3/4", find the "happy medium" and make them each 7/8".*
- The space between each dart should measure 1 ¼".
- Front dart length is 3 ½" long.

BACK:
- Measure the width of each dart and make sure they are the same. If not, equalize them *EX: if one is 1" and the other 3/4", find the "happy medium" and make them each 7/8".*
- The space between each dart should measure 1 ¼".
- Front dart length is 5 ½" long.

*Make sure that each dart is "centered" as shown.

Basic Fitted Skirt

TRUEING THE SKIRT DRAPES

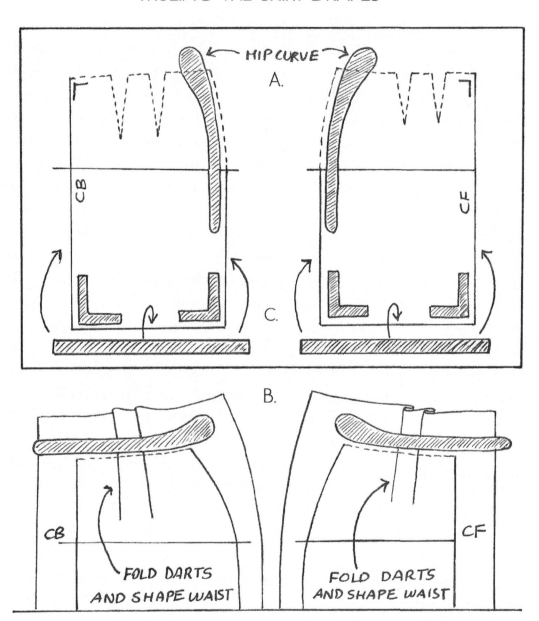

A. True/Smooth the curve from hip to waist using the Hip Curve ruler.
B. True the waist by closing/folding the darts and making sure the waist is a smooth line.
C. True the side seams and hems by making sure those lines are straight.

Basic Fitted Skirt

TRUEING THE SKIRT DRAPES

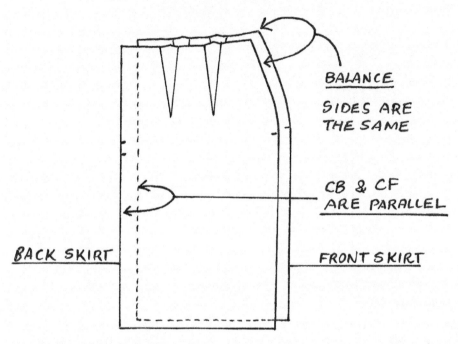

BALANCE

SIDES ARE
THE SAME

CB & CF
ARE PARALLEL

BACK SKIRT

FRONT SKIRT

The final step for Trueing is balancing:
• Place the FRONT skirt on top of the BACK skirt pattern (or visa versa)
  lining them up at the hip/side seam.

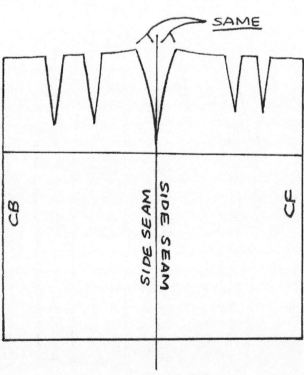

SAME

CB

SIDE SEAM

SIDE SEAM

CF

Once you have done this:
• Make sure the side seam/hip lines are
  EXACTLY the same for the FRONT and
  BACK.
• Check the CF and CB of the patterns
  and make sure they are PARALLEL to
  each other underneath, in other words,
  that they are "balanced".

Basic Fitted Skirt

ADD SEAM ALLOWANCE:

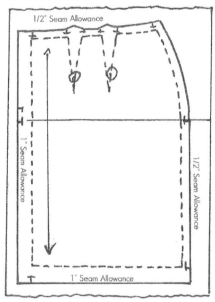
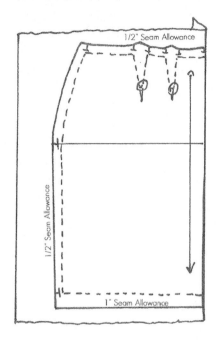

PIN MUSLIN DRAPE TO DRESS FORM:

- After draping the muslin pieces, trueing and adding seam allowance; pin both pieces together as shown in image below.
- Make sure all seams and darts are pinned properly with pins horizontally.
- Front and side seam pins face toward CF; back pins face toward CB.

45.

PRINCESS SEAM BODICE

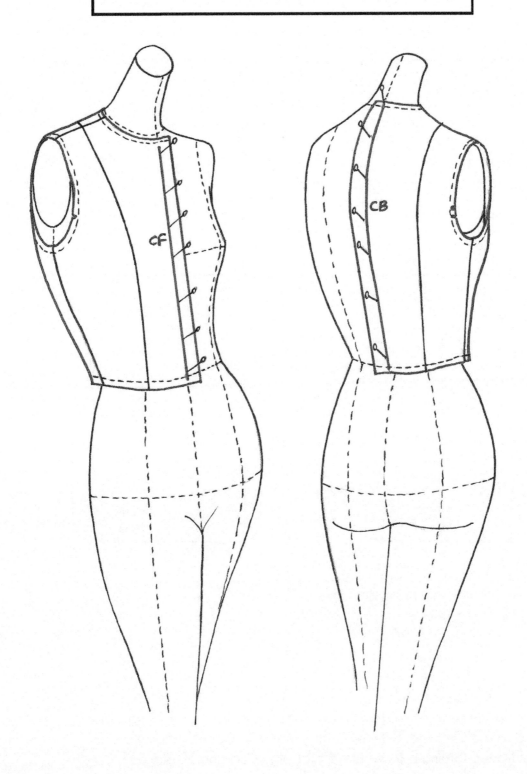

Princess Seam Bodice

PREPARING THE MUSLIN

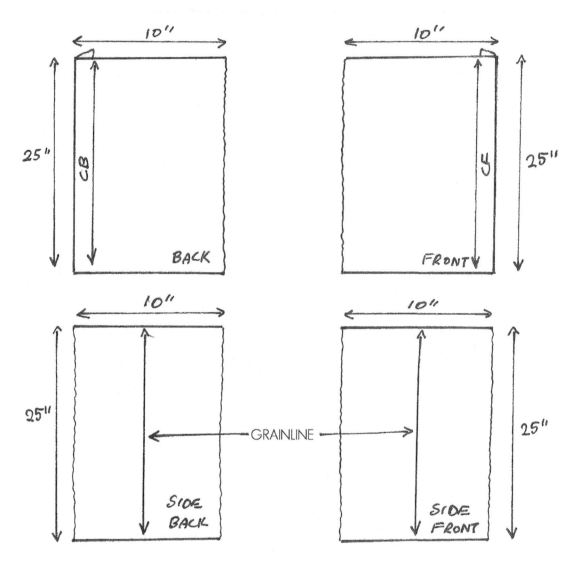

- Cut 4 pieces of muslin
- Each piece should be 25" Long x 10" Wide
- Label each piece:
    - CF (center front)
    - CB (center back)
    - SB (side back)
    - SF (side front)
- Fold the Center Front and Center Back pieces over 1" lengthwise
- Draw a Grainline 1" away from the fold line for CF and CB
- Draw a Grainline down the center of the SB and SF pieces

Princess Seam Bodice

PREPARING THE MUSLIN

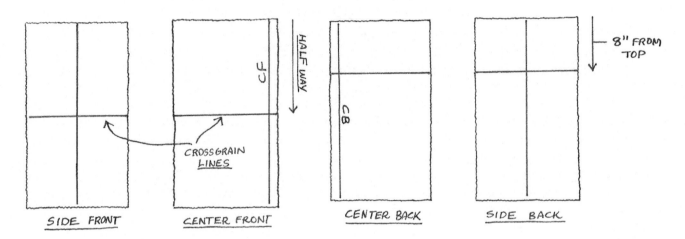

- On the CENTER FRONT and SIDE FRONT muslin pieces, draw horizontal (crosswise) grainlines in the center of both panels, as shown.

- On the CENTER BACK and SIDE BACK muslin pieces, draw horizontal (crosswise) grainlines 8" from the top of the fabric edge, as shown.

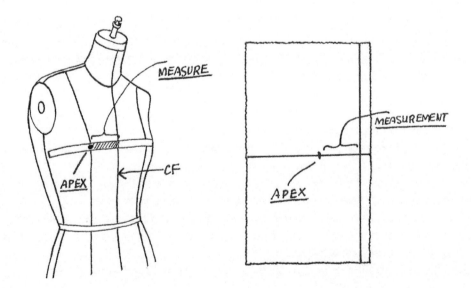

Once you have done this, go back to your FRONT panel, and Crossmark the APEX. Follow these steps:
- Measure the Dress Form from CF to the APEX (highest point of the BUST). *This measurement can differ from Dress Form to Dress Form, when it comes to sizes.*
- Crosmark the APEX on the CENTER FRONT panel (on the crossgrain line) by using the distance that you just measured.

Now you can begin draping the Basic Princess Bodice!

Princess Seam Bodice

FRONT

FRONT PRINCESS:

1.
- Pin the apex crossmark on the fabric to the apex position on the dress form.
- Make sure the crossgrain line of the fabric is on the bustline of the dress form, as shown.
- Pin the CF grainline fold of the fabric to the CF position of the dress form, making sure to pin at the CF neck as well as CF waist.

2.
- Drape the neckline by trimming the excess fabric around neck and then by clipping in small 1" intervals to the neckline of the dress form. Pin fabric on neckline as you clip. Clip and pin up to the neckline/shoulder position.
- Drape and smooth the fabric over the shoulder seam of the dress form. Pin in place.
- Now go to the waist area. Drape and smooth fabric from CF to just past the princess seam and pin in place.

3.
- Mark all the key areas of your front princess drape. Draw broken lines or dots on:
  - Neckline • Shoulder • Princess Seam • Waistline
- Crossmark 1 ½" above apex and 1 ½" below apex.
- Crossmark all the corners: CF neckline, neckline/shoulder, shoulder/princess, waist/princess, CF waist.

SIDE FRONT PRINCESS:

4.
- Pin the grainline of the side front panel (up & down), to the center of the front princess panel on the dress form.
- When doing this, make sure the crossgrain line of the cut fabric is on the bustline level of the dress form. Pin into place at the bustline and waist.

5.
- Clip to the waist to aid in draping and smoothing.
- Smooth fabric past the side seam, pinning at the waist/side seam as well as side seam/bustline.

6.
- Smooth and drape fabric up, over the bust, princess seam and shoulder seam.
- You'll notice the straight (up and down) grainline will shift to the right, toward the neckline if you drape correctly.
- At the middle of the arm plate (screw level), create ¼" pinch (see where lower arrow is pointing). This allows for ease so it does not feel tight across the chest.
- Pin at the neck/shoulder position as well as shoulder tip to help hold the fabric down.

7.
- Smooth and pin the princess seam in place.
- Trim excess fabric past the princess seam and clip up to but not through the princess seam (especially around bust curve area), to help in the smoothing and draping, as you pin in place.

8.
- Mark all the key areas of the fabric drape using short broken lines (or dotted marks):
  - Shoulder • Side Seam • Waist • Princess Seam
- Crossmark the following:
  - Shoulder tip/edge • 1" below armplate (underarm mark) • 1 ½" above the apex and 1 ½" below the apex
- Crossmark any cross points (perpendicular "corners"; two lines that intersect at right angles) including:
  - waist/side seam • waist/princess seam • shoulder/princess seam

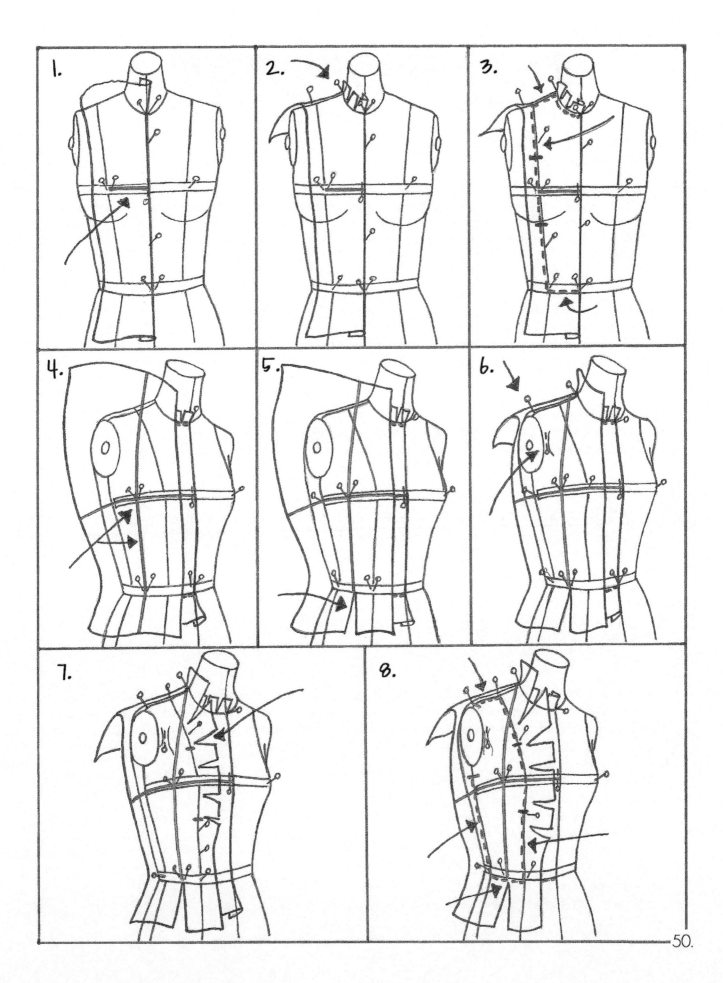

Princess Seam Bodice

BACK

CENTER BACK PRINCESS:

1.
- Pin the CB grainline fold of the fabric to the CB position of the dress form. Begin placing pins at the CB neck, then down the CB, ending with pins at the waist.
- Align the crossgrain line of the fabric to the shoulder blade level of the dress form. Pin in place at the princess seam.

2.
- Drape and smooth the back neckline. Carefully trim excess fabric at the neck area (but make sure not to over trim).
- Clip into the neckline, up to the neck but NOT THROUGH it. Pin into place.
- After clipping and pinning neckline, smooth fabric past the shoulder, and pin at the shoulder/princess position.

3.
- Mark CB, neckline, shoulder, princess seam and waist, using small broken lines or dotted marks.
- Crossmark any cross points (perpendicular "corners"; two lines that intersect at right angles):
  - CB neck • neckline/shoulder • shoulder/princess • waist/princess • CB waist

SIDE BACK PRINCESS:

4.
- Pin the grainline of the side back panel to the center of the back princess panel on the dress form.
- Match the crossgrain of the side back princess panel fabric to the shoulder blade level of the dress form (liken you did in the previous CB princess panel drape).
- Pin at the shoulder blade level, waist (at the center of the side back princess panel), and side seam.

5.
- Clip at the waist as shown, making sure not to over-clip through the waist. This will help the smoothing/draping in that area.

6.
- Smooth the side back princess panel (fabric) past the shoulder; you will notice that the straight grainline (in the middle) will shift toward the neckline if you smooth properly. Pin at the neckline and shoulder tip.
- Drape and smooth fabric past the princess seam of the dress form and pin into place on the princess seam.

7.
- Mark the shoulder, princess, waist & side seam
- Mark the middle of the arm plate, at the arm plate screw level
- Crossmark any cross points (perpendicular "corners"; two lines that intersect at right angles):
  - shoulder/princess
  - shoulder tip
  - waist/princess
  - waist/side seam
  - 1" below arm plate

51.

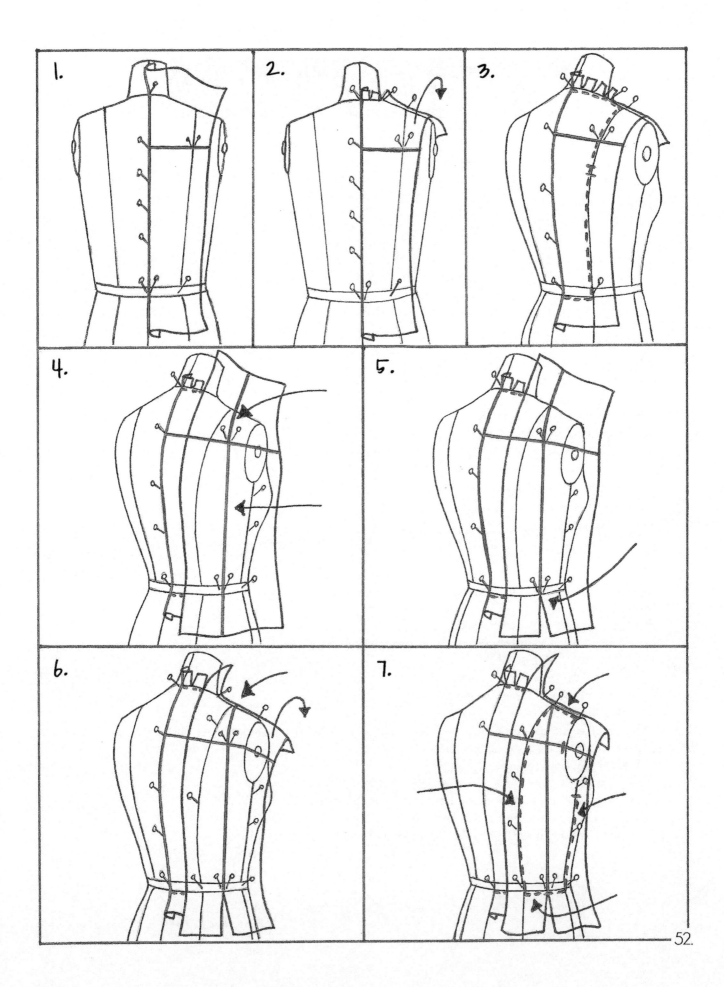

Princess Seam Bodice

TRUEING INSTRUCTIONS

CENTER FRONT:

1.
- After draping the CF Princess Seam Bodice Drape, neatly lay on Dotted Paper, making sure the CF grainline is aligned to the "straight/up-and-down grain" of the Dotted Paper.
- Tape down lightly or pin so it stays in place.
- Trace Drape onto Dotted Paper using the Tracing Wheel.

2.
- Using straight ruler to straighten the following:
    o Shoulder, Waist
- Use the French Curve to shape NECKLINE correctly.
- SMOOTH the Princess Seam using the Vary Form Curve Ruler or the straight ruler. Just make sure the seam is smooth and not "choppy".
- Make sure these corners are at a 90-degree angle:
    o CF Neckline, CF Waist.
    o Princess Seam at Shoulder and Waist.

SIDE FRONT:

3.
- After draping the Side Front Princess Seam Bodice Drape, neatly lay on Dotted Paper, making sure the grainline in the middle of the draped pattern is aligned to the "straight/up-and-down grain" of the Dotted Paper.
- Tape down lightly or pin so it stays in place.
- Trace Drape onto Dotted Paper using the Tracing Wheel.

4.
- Using straight ruler to straighten the following:
    o Shoulder, Side Seam.
- SMOOTH the Princess Seam using the Vary Form Curve Ruler or the straight ruler. Just make sure the curved area around the bust is smooth and not "choppy".
- SMOOTH the Waist seam.
- Make sure these corners are at a 90-degree angle:
    o Princess Seam at Shoulder, and at the Princess Seam Waist.
    o Shoulder Tip at the top of the Armhole.
    o Side Seam at the bottom of the Armhole, and at the Side Seam Waist.

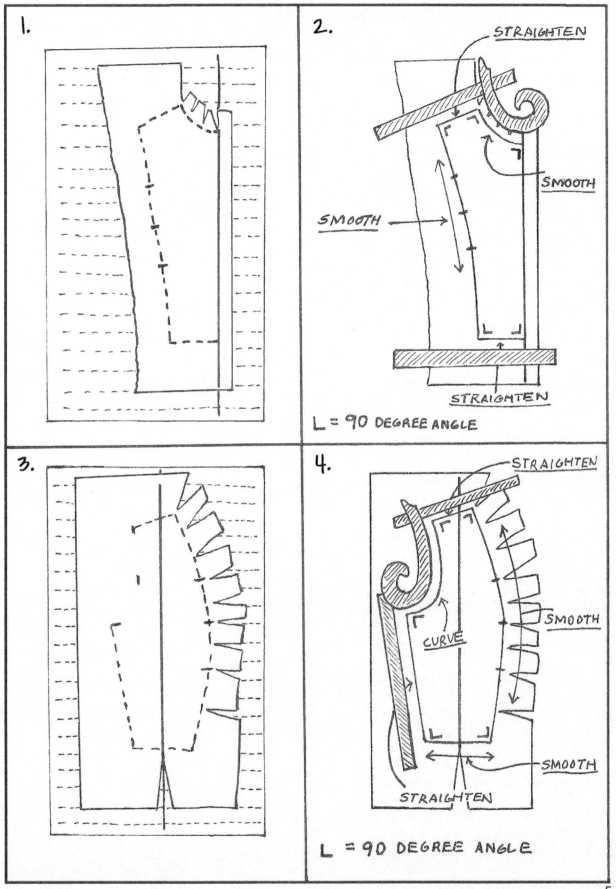

1.

2. STRAIGHTEN

SMOOTH

SMOOTH

STRAIGHTEN

L = 90 DEGREE ANGLE

3.

4. STRAIGHTEN

CURVE

SMOOTH

SMOOTH

STRAIGHTEN

L = 90 DEGREE ANGLE

Princess Seam Bodice

TRUEING INSTRUCTIONS

CENTER BACK:

5.
- After draping the CB Princess Seam Bodice Drape, neatly lay on Dotted Paper, making sure the CB grainline is aligned to the "straight/up-and-down grain" of the Dotted Paper.
- Tape down lightly or pin so it stays in place.
- Trace Drape onto Dotted Paper using the Tracing Wheel.

6.
- Using straight ruler to straighten the following:
  - o Shoulder, Waist
- Use the French Curve to shape NECKLINE correctly.
- SMOOTH the Princess Seam using the Vary Form Curve Ruler or the straight ruler. Just make sure the seam is smooth and not "choppy".
- Make sure these corners are at a 90-degree angle:
  - o CB Neckline, CB Waist
  - o Princess Seam at Shoulder and Waist

SIDE BACK:

7.
- After draping the Side Back Princess Seam Bodice Drape, neatly lay on Dotted Paper, making sure the grainline in the middle of the draped pattern is aligned to the "straight/up-and-down grain" of the Dotted Paper.
- Tape down lightly or pin so it stays in place.
- Trace Drape onto Dotted Paper using the Tracing Wheel.

8.
- Using straight ruler to straighten the following:
  - o Shoulder, Side Seam.
- SMOOTH the Princess Seam using the Vary Form Curve Ruler or the straight ruler. Just make sure the curve is smooth and not "choppy".
- SMOOTH the Waist seam
- Make sure these corners are at a 90-degree angle:
  - o Princess Seam at Shoulder, and at the Princess Seam Waist.
  - o Shoulder Tip at the top of the Armhole.
  - o Side Seam at the bottom of the Armhole, and at the Side Seam Waist.

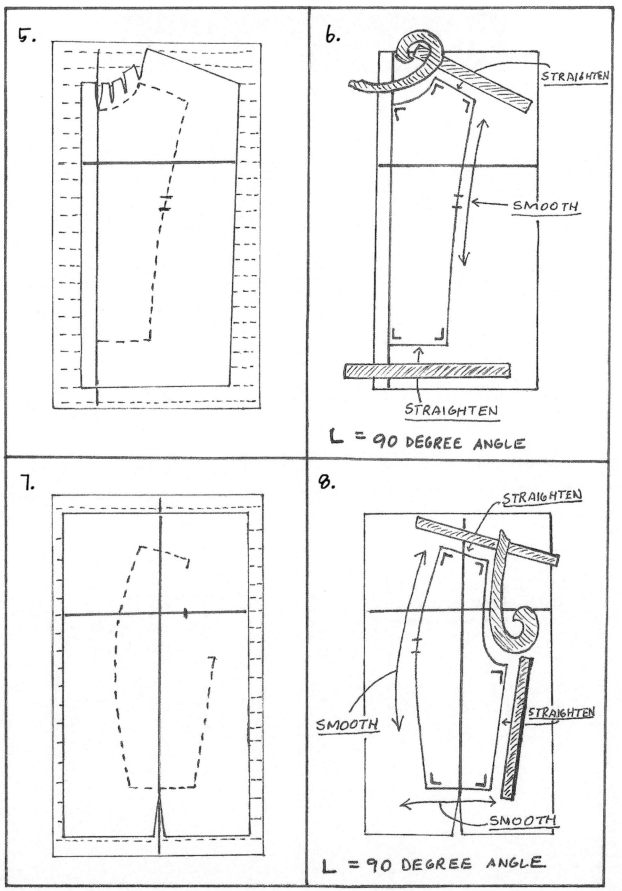

5.

6.

STRAIGHTEN

SMOOTH

STRAIGHTEN

L = 90 DEGREE ANGLE

7.

8.

STRAIGHTEN

SMOOTH

STRAIGHTEN

SMOOTH

L = 90 DEGREE ANGLE

Princess Seam Bodice

SEAM ALLOWANCE & NOTCHES

1.

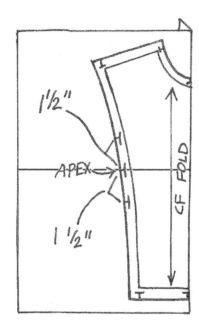

2.

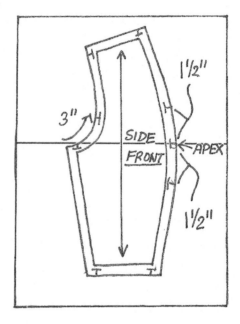

CENTER FRONT

- Remove the draped piece from the form and lie flat.
- Add ½" seam allowance to princess seam, shoulder seam & waist seam.
- Add ¼" seam allowance to neckline.
- Draw notches at CF neckline, CF waist, Princess Seam at Shoulder, Princess Seam at waist & Shoulder Seam at neck.
- Draw notch at the Apex and add notches 1 ½" above and 1 ½" below the Apex.

SIDE FRONT

- Remove the draped piece from the form and lie flat.
- Add ½" seam allowance to all seams.
- Draw notches at Princess Seam Shoulder, Princess Seam Waist, Armhole Shoulder & Side Seam (armhole & waist).
- Draw Armhole notch 3" up from Side Seam.
- Draw notch at the Apex and add notches 1 ½" above and 1 ½" below the Apex.

Princess Seam Bodice

SEAM ALLOWANCE & NOTCHES

3.

1" C.B. SEAM ALLOWANCE

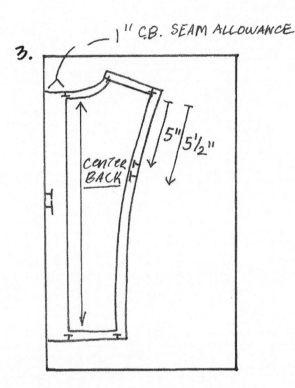

CENTER BACK

5" 5½"

4.

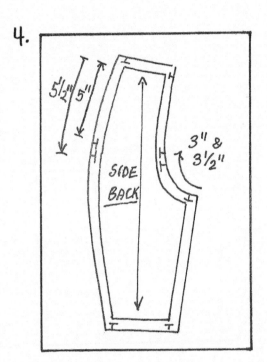

5½" 5"

SIDE BACK

3" & 3½"

CENTER BACK

- Remove the draped piece from the form and lie flat.
- Add ½" seam allowance to princess seam, shoulder seam & waist seam.
- Add ¼" seam allowance to neckline.
- Add 1" seam allowance to center back seam.
- Draw notches at CB neckline, CB waist, Princess Seam at Shoulder, Princess Seam at waist & Shoulder Seam at neck.
- Draw 2 notches at Princess Seam. 5" and 5 1/2" down from the shoulder.

SIDE BACK

- Remove the draped piece from the form and lie flat.
- Add ½" seam allowance to all seams.
- Draw notches at Princess Seam Shoulder, Princess Seam Waist, Armhole Shoulder & Side Seam (armhole & waist).
- Draw 2 Armhole notches 3" and 3 1/2" up from Side Seam.
- Draw 2 notches at Princess Seam. 5" and 5 1/2" down from the shoulder.

58.

Princess Seam Bodice

TRUED WITH SEAM ALLOWANCE
AND PINNED ON DRESS FORM

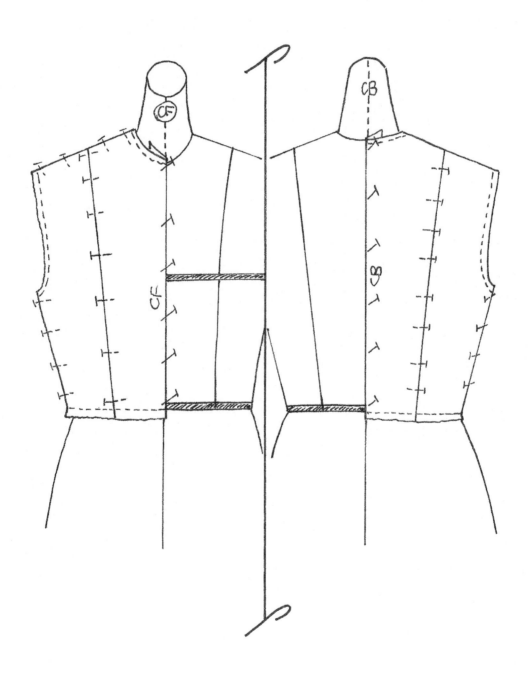

Princess Seam Bodice

SEWING INSTRUCTIONS

- After draping the Princess Seam Bodice and trueing the draped pieces onto Dotted Paper, cut pattern pieces with seam allowances on Muslin.
- Cut TWO pieces of:
  - Center Back
  - Side Back
  - Side Front
- Cut ONE piece of:
  - Center Front

- Sew Side Front pieces to the Center Front along the Princess Seams.
- Make sure to "clip" at the bust area to release tension and allow seam to curve.
- Press seams open.

Princess Seam Bodice
SEWING INSTRUCTIONS

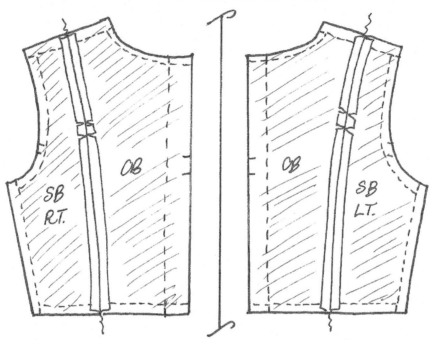

- Sew Center Back and Side Back pieces together at the Princess Seams.
- Make sure to "clip" at the bust area to release tension and allow seam to curve.
- Press seams open.

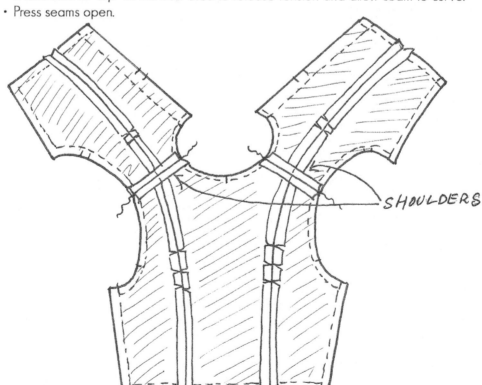

SHOULDERS

- Sew Front Shoulders to Back Shoulders, making sure Princess Seams MATCH! Press seams open.

Princess Seam Bodice

SEWING INSTRUCTIONS

- Sew Front Side Seams to Back Side Seams, both on the right and left sides.
- Press seams open.

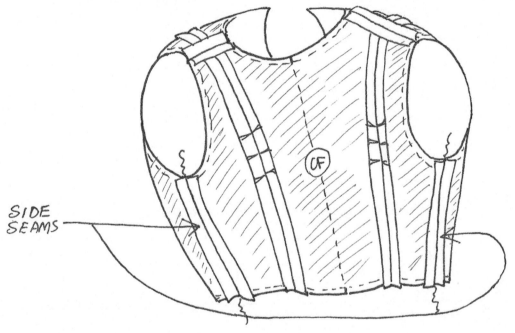

SIDE SEAMS

- Sew a stay-stitch 1/4" away from edge at the Neckline, Armholes and Hem.
- Press the entire bodice and put on the dress form, pinning the back closed at 1".

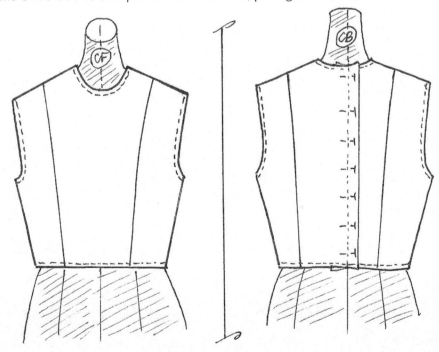

MIDRIFF TOP W/ PEPLUM

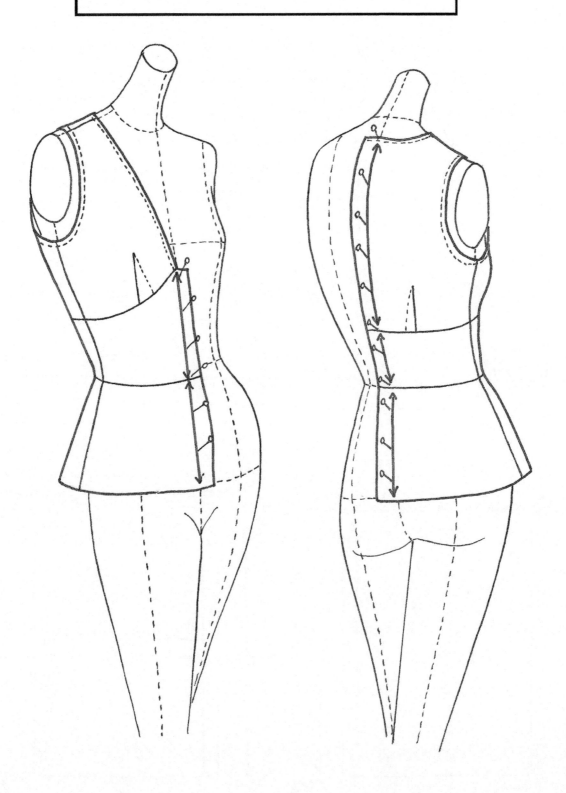

Midriff Top w/ Peplum

PREPARING THE MUSLIN

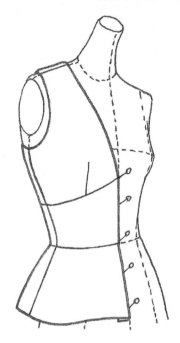 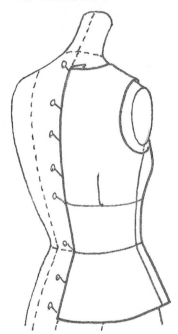

I. TOP

FRONT:
- Cut a piece of muslin 18" L x 14" W
- Draw a vertical grainline 1" away from edge.
- Label this piece "CF" for Front

BACK:
- Cut a piece of muslin 17" L x 12" W
- Draw a vertical grainline 1" away from left side edge.
- Label this piece "CB" for Back.
- Draw a crossgrain (horizontal) line 8" below the top edge. Label this line SHOULDER BLADE.

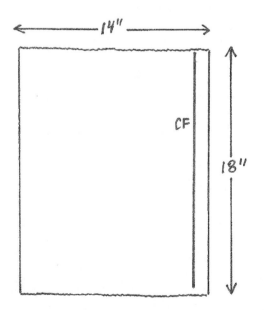 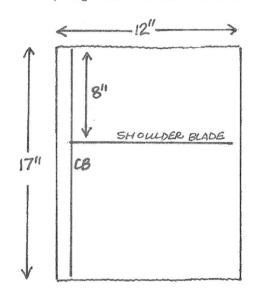

Midriff Top w/ Peplum

PREPARING THE MUSLIN

2. MIDRIFF

FRONT:
- Cut a square piece of muslin 12" x 12"
- Draw a vertical grainline 1" away from right side edge.
- Label this piece "CF" for Front

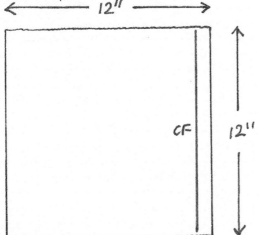

BACK:
- Cut a square piece of muslin 10" x 10"
- Draw a vertical grainline 1" away from left side edge.
- Label this piece "CB" for Back.

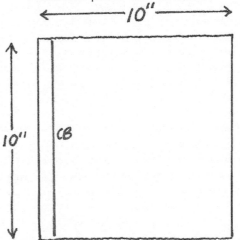

3. PEPLUM

FRONT:
- Cut a square piece of muslin 13" x 13"
- Draw a vertical grainline 1" away from right side edge.
- Label this piece "CF" for Front.
- Draw a crossmark 5" from the top edge of the cut muslin at the vertical grainline.
- Label this "CF WAIST".

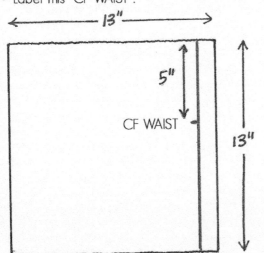

BACK:
- Cut a square piece of muslin 13" x 13"
- Draw a vertical grainline 1" away from left side edge.
- Label this piece "CB" for Back.
- Draw a crossmark 5" from the top edge of the cut muslin at the vertical grainline.
- Label this "CB WAIST".

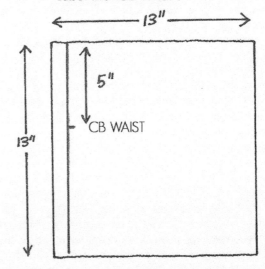

Midriff Top w/ Peplum

TOP: FRONT

- Before you begin draping, mark the preferred style lines on the dress form. You case use draping/marking tape or if this tape is not available, you can cut thin strips of muslin and pin them to the dress form following your preferred style lines.
- You can also use pins to mark the style lines directly on the form.

1.

- After prepping the fabric for the drape, begin by placing the pre-cut piece of fabric on the form and pinning the folded edge to the front neckline.
- Make sure when pinning to leave about 3-4" of muslin beyond the shoulders at the top, as shown.

2.

- Drape the fabric over the shoulder and place pins at the shoulder.
- Cut and tear any excess fabric at the shoulder, leaving at least 1 ½"-2" extra.
- Cut any extra fabric at the midriff area, leaving about 3" below your marked style lines.

3.

- Smooth and drape the armhole area and pin. Clip fabric as shown to help in smoothing the area.
- Smooth and pin to the underarm/armpit mark (1" below armplate).

4.

- Smooth fabric past the side seam, pinning as you drape and smooth.
- If you have draped this area properly, it will create a smooth side bust.
- Notice the excess fabric that is around the princess area; this will be folded into a dart.

5.

- Drape the lower part of your top, following the style lines on the dress form.
- Smooth and pin, clipping along the way to help.
- Smooth from the side seam to the princess and draw a crossmark (this will be one side of the dart), then smooth and pin from CF to the princess, draw a crossmark at the princess (this will be the other side of the dart.
- Fold the dart right under the bust at the princess line. Always put the fold ON THE PRINCESS LINE, and the dart will fold toward the front.

6.

- Mark all the style lines.
- Mark the shoulder, neckline, side seam and midriff area.
- Crossmark any corners:
    - o Front/shoulder
    - o Shoulder/armhole
    - o Side seam/underarm-armpit
    - o Side seam/midriff
    - o CF/midriff

7.

- When you remove drape from dress form, fabric should look like image.

67.

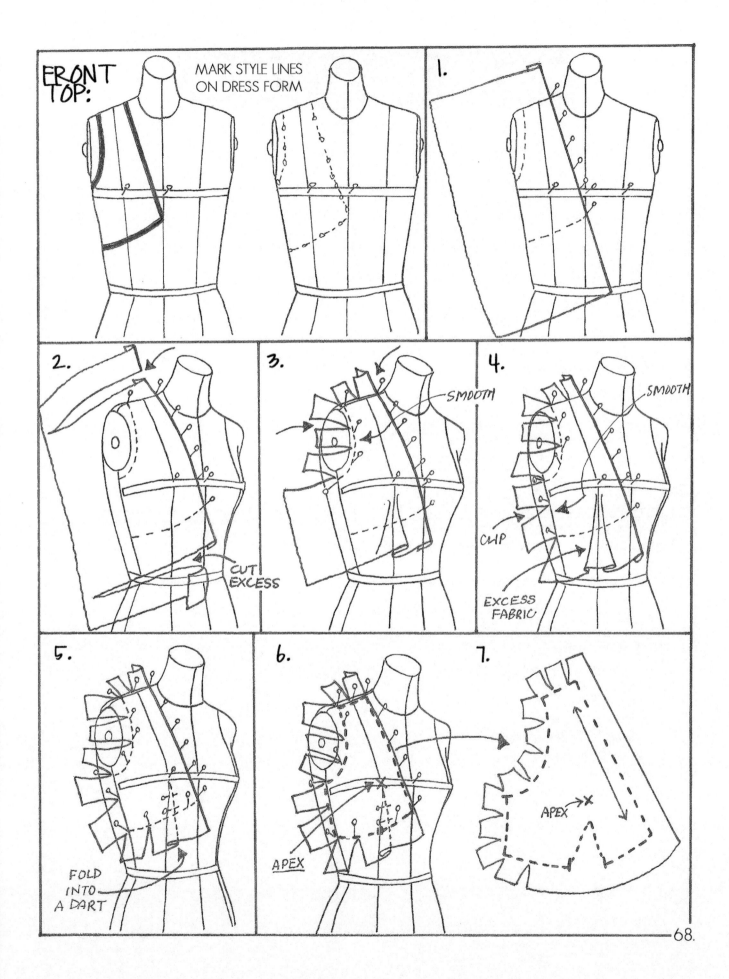

FRONT TOP: MARK STYLE LINES ON DRESS FORM

1.

2. CUT EXCESS

3. SMOOTH

4. SMOOTH / CLIP / EXCESS FABRIC

5. FOLD INTO A DART

6. APEX

7. APEX → X

68.

Midriff Top w/ Peplum

TOP: BACK

- Mark the preferred style lines on the dress form. You case use Draping/marking Tape or if this tape is not available, you can cut thin strips of muslin and pin to the dress form following your preferred style lines.
- You can also use pins to mark the style lines directly on the form.

1.
- Pin the cut & prepared piece of fabric marked CB onto the CB of the dress form. Place folded edge at the CB.
- When pinning, place crossgrain line at the shoulder blade level of the dress form, approximately 4 ½" below the CB neck point.
- Continue to pin along the crossgrain line.

2.
- Drape and smooth at the neckline area. Clip to help the smoothing process and pin as you drape.
- Smooth the fabric past the shoulder and pin the shoulder area.

3.
- Drape the armhole area. Clip fabric as shown up to BUT NOT THROUGH the style lines (or pins) that you placed to mark the back armhole of your top.
- Pin the back armhole after you have clipped and smoothed the fabric.
- Smooth drape past the side seam and pin at the side seam.
- Pin at the back midriff, clipping to help smooth that area.

4.
- Mark all the style lines.
- Mark the back neckline, shoulder, armhole, side seam and back midriff.
- Crossmark all corners:
    o CB neck
    o Neckline/shoulder
    o Shoulder/underarm-armpit
    o Side seam/midriff
    o CB midriff

BACK TOP:

MARK STYLE LINES
ON DRESS FORM

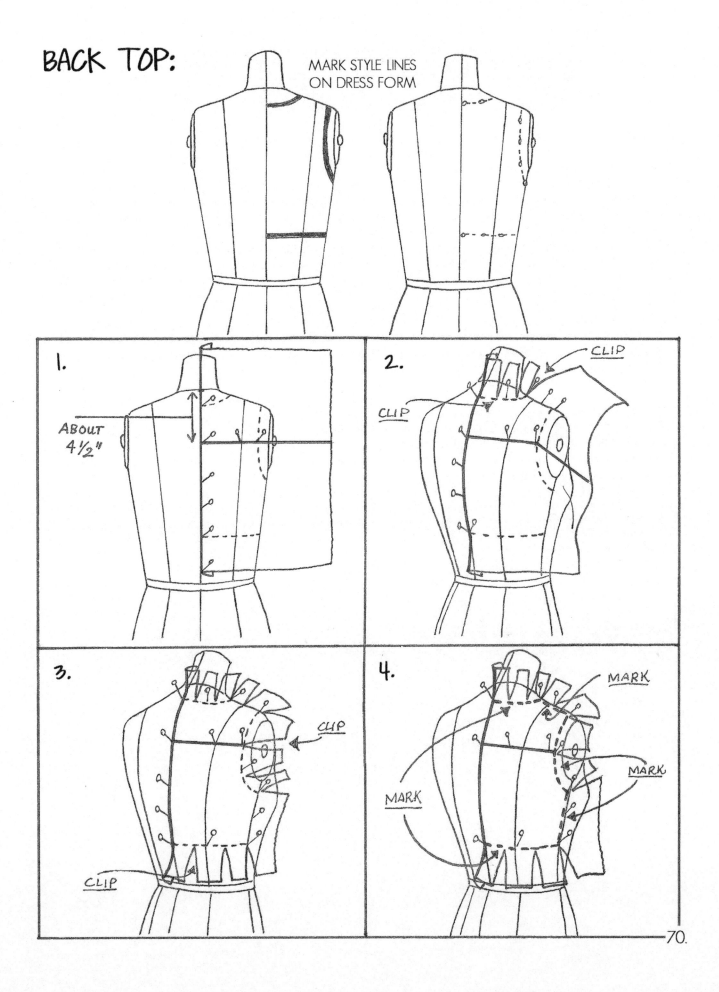

1.

ABOUT
4½"

2.

CLIP

CLIP

3.

CLIP

CLIP

4.

MARK

MARK

MARK

70.

Midriff Top w/ Peplum
FRONT MIDRIFF

- Mark the preferred style lines on the dress form. You case use Draping/marking Tape or if this tape is not available, you can cut thin strips of muslin and pin to the dress form following your preferred style lines.
- You can also use pins to mark the style lines directly on the form.

1.
- Pin pre-cut fabric to the CF of the dress form at the midriff area, placing folded edge at the CF.
- Make sure to leave at least 2" of extra fabric at the top and 2" of extra fabric at the bottom so you have enough fabric to drape the midriff section.

2.
- Drape the waist area.
- Smooth fabric at the waist, from CF to side seam.
- Clip to the waist as shown to help in smoothing the waist area.
- Pin at the waist and side seam.

3.
- Drape fabric past the side seam, making sure the midriff/abdomen area is smooth. Make sure not to drape too tightly. Pin the side seam.
- Smooth fabric at the underbust/midriff and pin fabric to the dress form. Clip the fabric as shown to help with the smoothing.

4.
- Mark all the style lines of your midriff section.
- Mark the underbust/midriff, the waist, and the side seam.
- Crossmark all corners:
  - o Side seam/underbust
  - o Side seam/waist
  - o CF waist

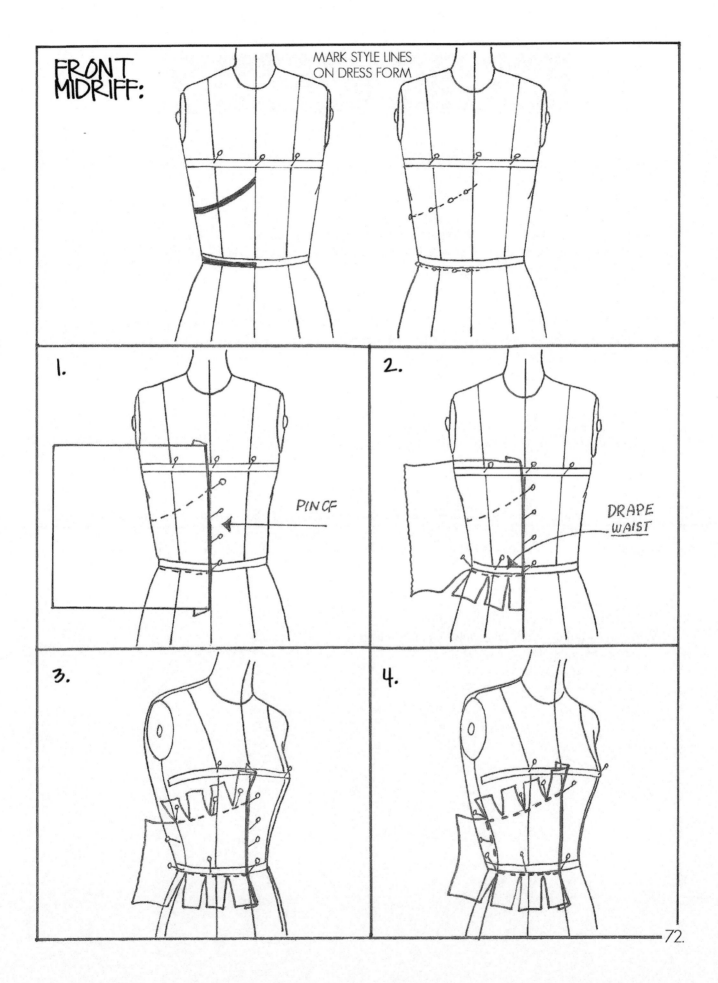

FRONT MIDRIFF:

MARK STYLE LINES ON DRESS FORM

1.

PIN CF

2.

DRAPE WAIST

3.

4.

Midriff Top w/ Peplum

BACK MIDRIFF

- Mark the preferred style lines on the dress form. You can use Draping/marking Tape or if this tape is not available, you can cut thin strips of muslin and pin to the dress form following your preferred style lines.
- You can also use pins to mark the style lines directly on the form.

1.
- Pin pre-cut fabric to the CF of the dress form at the midriff area, placing folded edge at the CF.
- Make sure to leave at least 2" of extra fabric at the top and 2" of extra fabric at the bottom so you have enough fabric to drape the midriff section.

2.
- Drape the waist area.
- Smooth fabric at the waist, from CF to side seam.
- Clip to the waist as shown to help in smoothing the waist area.
- Pin at the waist and side seam.

3.
- Drape fabric past the side seam, making sure the midriff/abdomen area is smooth. Make sure not to drape too tightly. Pin the side seam.
- Smooth fabric at the underbust/midriff and pin fabric to the dress form. Clip the fabric as shown to help with the smoothing.

4.
- Mark all the style lines of your midriff section.
- Mark the underbust/midriff, the waist, and the side seam.
- Crossmark all corners:
    o Side seam/underbust
    o Side seam/waist
    o CF waist

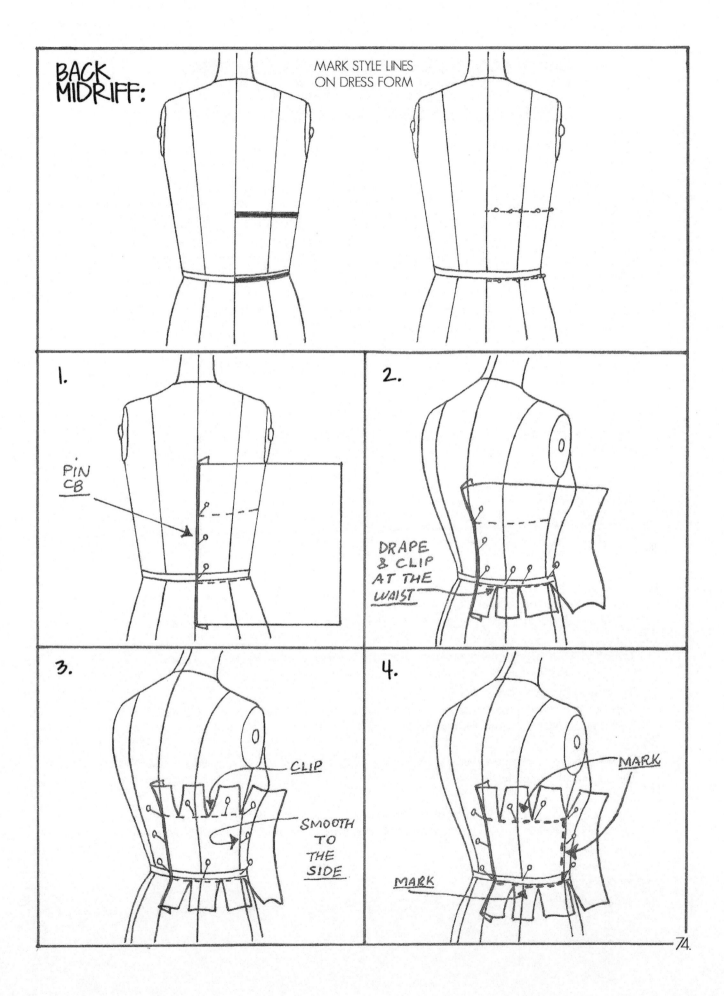

BACK MIDRIFF:

MARK STYLE LINES ON DRESS FORM

1.

PIN CB

2.

DRAPE & CLIP AT THE WAIST

3.

CLIP

SMOOTH TO THE SIDE

4.

MARK

MARK

74.

Midriff Top w/ Peplum

FRONT PEPLUM

1.
- Place pre-cut muslin/fabric at CF of the dress form.
- Pin folded edge to the CF of the dress form, placing the 5" crossmark at the CF waist.

2.
- Drape the waist by smoothing the fabric from the CF waist to the side seam, clipping and pinning while smoothing the fabric.
- Pin to the side seam/waist position.
- While you are doing this, make sure you are creating a slight flare at the side. You do not want the peplum to be tight but more like small a flared "skirt".

3.
- Once you have established your preferred amount of flare in your front peplum, pin the fabric at the side seam of the dress form.

4.
- Finish by marking the style lines including the waist, side seam and the hem.
- For the hem, you can "eye it" by drawing short lines parallel to the bottom of the dress form.
- Crossmark any corners:
    - o CF waist
    - o Side seam/waist
    - o Side seam/hem
    - o CF hem

BACK PEPLUM

1.
- Place pre-cut muslin/fabric at CB of the dress form.
- Pin folded edge to the CB of the dress form, placing the 5" crossmark at the CB waist.

2.
- Drape the waist by smoothing the fabric from the CB waist to the side seam, clipping and pinning while smoothing the fabric.
- Pin to the side seam/waist position.
- While you are doing this, make sure you are creating a slight flare at the side. You do not want the peplum to be tight but more like a small flared "skirt".

3.
- Once you have established your preferred amount of flare in your front peplum, pin the fabric at the side seam of the dress form.

4.
- Finish by marking the style lines including the waist, side seam and the hem.
- For the hem, you can "eye it" by drawing short lines parallel to the bottom of the dress form.
- Crossmark any corners:
    - o CB waist
    - o Side seam/waist
    - o Side seam/hem
    - o CB hem

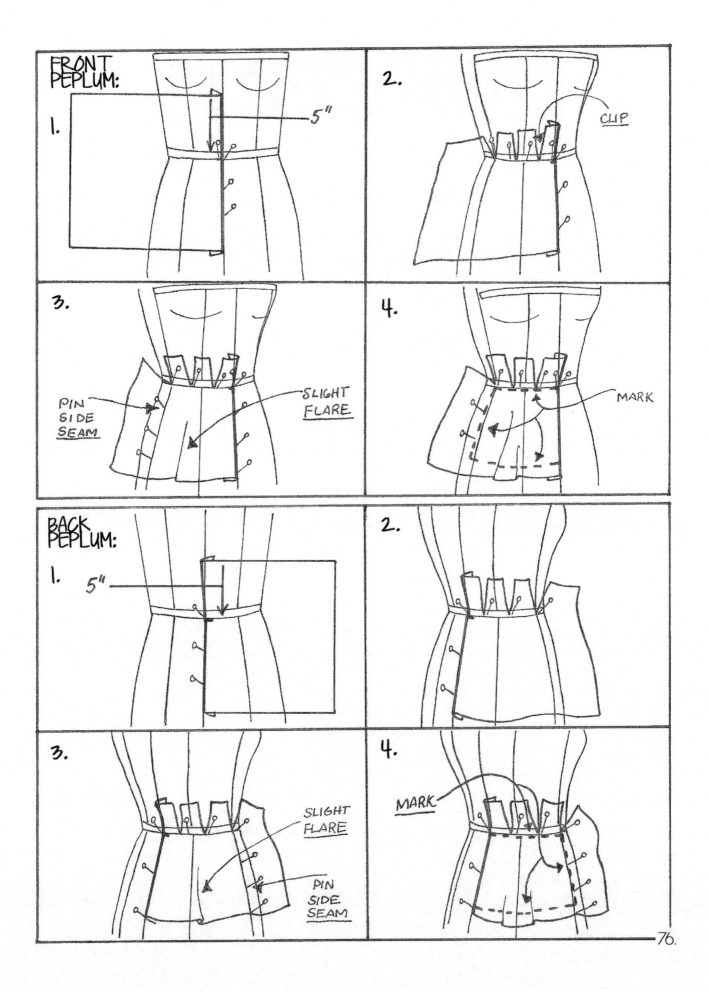

FRONT
PEPLUM:

1.

5"

2.

CLIP

3.

PIN
SIDE
SEAM

SLIGHT
FLARE

4.

MARK

BACK
PEPLUM:

1.

5"

2.

3.

SLIGHT
FLARE

PIN
SIDE
SEAM

4.

MARK

Midriff Top w/ Peplum

TRUEING

FRONT UPPER SECTION

1.
- After draping the Front Upper Section of the Waist Midriff Top, neatly lay on Dotted Paper, making sure the CF grainline is aligned to the "straight/up-and-down grain" of the Dotted Paper.
- Tape down lightly or pin so it stays in place.
- Trace Drape onto Dotted Paper using the Tracing Wheel.

2.
- Using a straight ruler to straighten the following:
    o Front Neckline, Shoulder, Side Seam
- Use the French Curve to shape the ARMHOLE correctly.
- SMOOTH the seam lines at the MIDRIFF (at the bottom); this can be done using a straight ruler and/or the Vary Form Curve ruler. Make sure the lines are continuous and smooth (not choppy).
- Make sure these corners are at a 90-degree angle:
    o Front Neckline at the Shoulder
    o Front Neckline at the Midriff seam.
    o Shoulder Tip at the top of the Armhole.
    o Side Seam at the bottom of the Armhole.
    o Side Seam at the Midriff seam.
- Draw the DART correctly by:
    o Make sure the Dart tip begins ½" BELOW the APEX (highest point of the bust).
    o Make sure the dart legs are the same measurement.

FRONT MIDRIFF

3.
- After draping the Front Midriff of the Waist Midriff Top, neatly lay on Dotted Paper, making sure the CF grainline is aligned to the "straight/up-and-down grain" of the Dotted Paper.
- Tape down lightly or pin so it stays in place.
- Trace Drape onto Dotted Paper using the Tracing Wheel.

4.
- Using a straight ruler to straighten the following:
    o CF/Center Front, Side Seam
- SMOOTH the seam lines at the MIDRIFF (at the top); this can be done using the Vary Form Curve ruler. Make sure the lines are continuous and smooth (not choppy).
- SMOOTH the WAIST using the Vary Form Curve ruler; making sure the waist line is not choppy.
- Make sure these corners are at a 90-degree angle:
    o CF, at the top Midriff and at the Waist.
    o Side Seam, at the Waist.

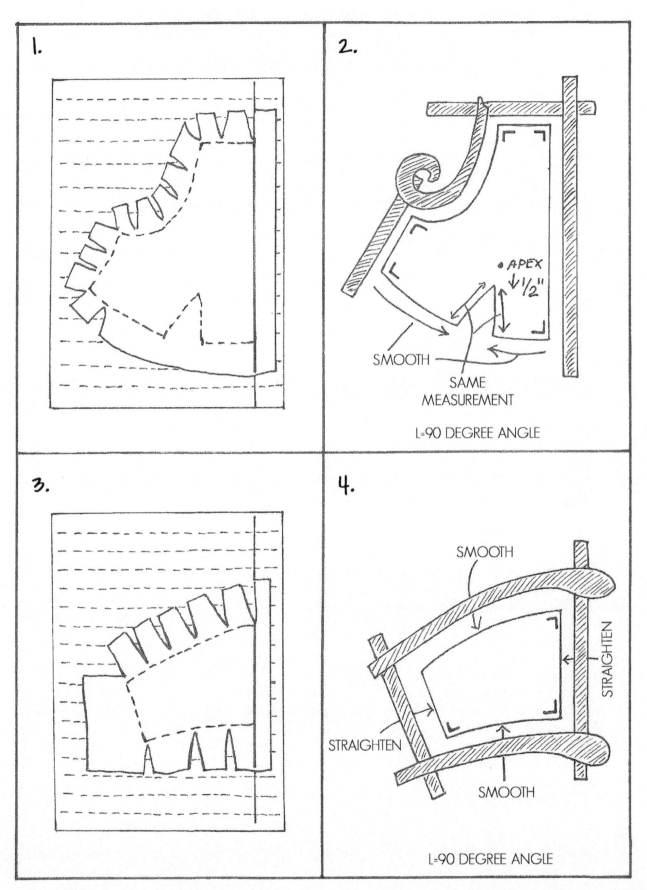

1.

2.

APEX

↓ 1/2"

SMOOTH

SAME
MEASUREMENT

L=90 DEGREE ANGLE

3.

4.

SMOOTH

STRAIGHTEN

STRAIGHTEN

SMOOTH

L=90 DEGREE ANGLE

Midriff Top w/ Peplum

TRUEING

BACK UPPER SECTION

5.

- After draping the Back Upper Section of the Waist Midriff Top, neatly lay on Dotted Paper, making sure the CB grainline is aligned to the "straight/up-and-down grain" of the Dotted Paper.
- Tape down lightly or pin so it stays in place.
- Trace Drape onto Dotted Paper using the Tracing Wheel.

6.

- Using a straight ruler to straighten the following:
    o CB/Center Back, Shoulder, Side Seam
- Using a French Curve, smooth NECKLINE, as well as the Armhole.
- SMOOTH the seam lines at the MIDRIFF (at the bottom); this can be done using the Vary Form Curve ruler. Make sure the lines are continuous and smooth (not choppy).
- Make sure these corners are at a 90-degree angle:
    o CB/Center Back at the Top Neckline, and Midriff (bottom).
    o Shoulder, at the Neckline, and Shoulder Tip.
    o Midriff, at the CB/Center Back, and the Side Seam.

BACK MIDRIFF

7.

- After draping the Back Midriff of the Waist Midriff Top, neatly lay on Dotted Paper, making sure the CB grainline is aligned to the "straight/up-and-down grain" of the Dotted Paper.
- Tape down lightly or pin so it stays in place.
- Trace Drape onto Dotted Paper using the Tracing Wheel.

8.

- Using a straight ruler to straighten the following:
    o CB/Center Back, Side Seam.
- SMOOTH the seam lines at the MIDRIFF (at the top); this can be done using the Vary Form Curve ruler. Make sure the lines are continuous and smooth (not choppy).
- SMOOTH the WAIST using the Vary Form Curve ruler; making sure the waist line is not choppy.
- Make sure these corners are at a 90-degree angle:
    o CB, at the top Midriff and at the Waist.
    o Side Seam, at the Midriff and the Waist.

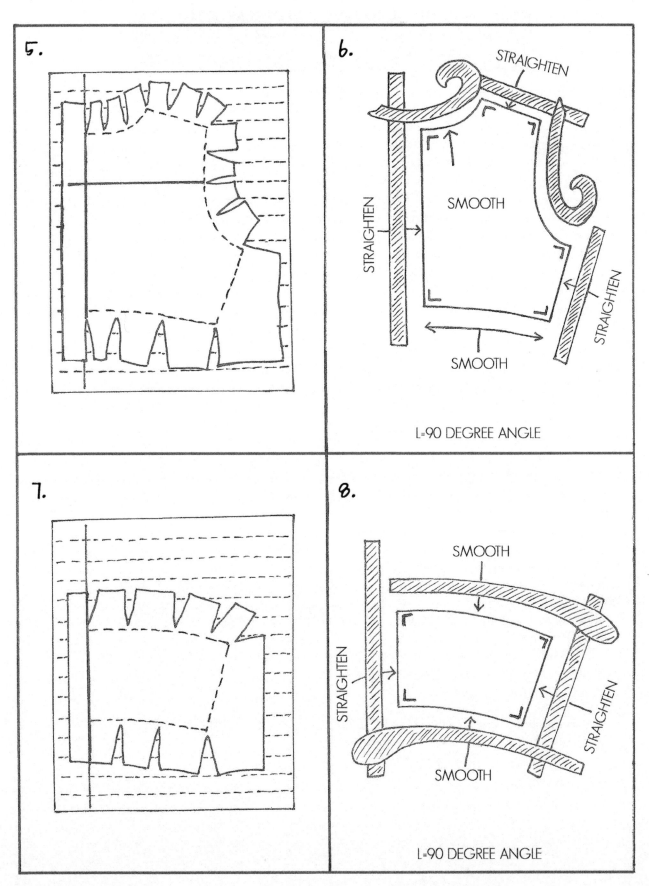

5.

6.

STRAIGHTEN

STRAIGHTEN

SMOOTH

STRAIGHTEN

SMOOTH

L=90 DEGREE ANGLE

7.

8.

SMOOTH

STRAIGHTEN

STRAIGHTEN

SMOOTH

L=90 DEGREE ANGLE

Midriff Top w/ Peplum

TRUEING

FRONT PEPLUM

9.
- After draping the Front Peplum of the Waist Midriff Top, neatly lay on Dotted Paper, making sure the CF grainline is aligned to the "straight/up-and-down grain" of the Dotted Paper.
- Tape down lightly or pin so it stays in place.
- Trace Drape onto Dotted Paper using the Tracing Wheel.

BACK PEPLUM

10.
- After draping the Back Peplum of the Waist Midriff Top, neatly lay on Dotted Paper, making sure the CB grainline is aligned to the "straight/up-and-down grain" of the Dotted Paper.
- Tape down lightly or pin so it stays in place.
- Trace Drape onto Dotted Paper using the Tracing Wheel.

BEFORE PROCEEDING WITH TRUEING, BALANCE THE SIDES OF THE PEPLUM DRAPES:

11.
- Place the FRONT PEPLUM traced pattern on top of the BACK PEPLUM traced pattern. Make sure:
  - o Match both pieces at the SIDE SEAM/WAIST corners

THEN:
  - o Make sure the CF and CB are PARALLEL to each other
  - o Check the SIDE SEAMS and the angles; if they are NOT the same (parallel to each other), then proceed to do the following steps:

12.
- Keeping both Pattern Pieces together, matching at the Side Seam/Waist and PARALLEL to each other at the CF and CB...
- SPLIT THE DIFFERENCE at the Side Seams, so that they are BOTH the same/parallel to each other, by adding to one and taking away from the other.

13.
- The image shows how both the FRONT and BACK Peplums are BALANCED, with:
  - o The Side Seams at the same angle.
  - o And the CF and CB are PARALLEL.

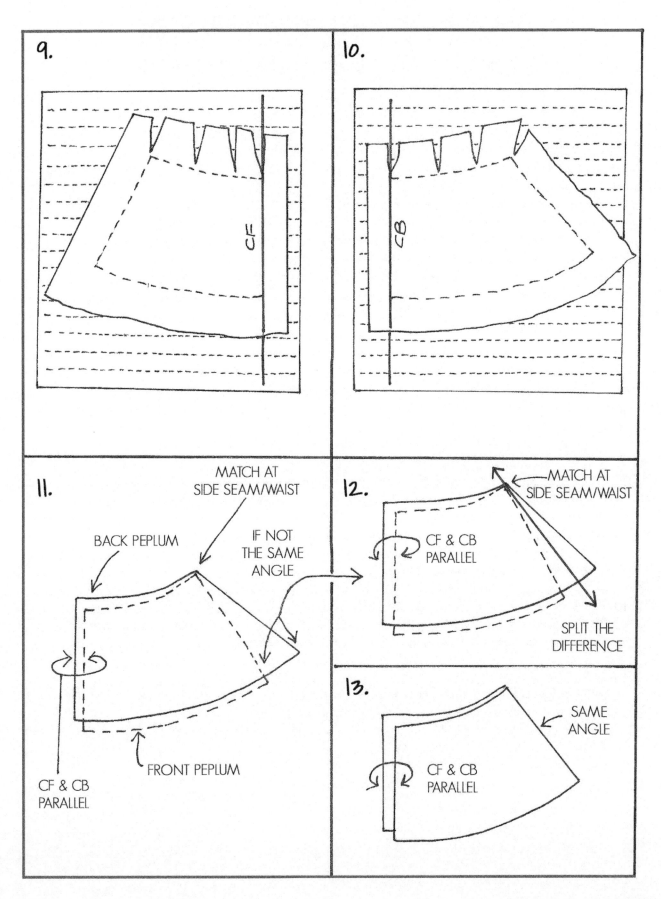

9.

CF

10.

CB

11.

MATCH AT
SIDE SEAM/WAIST

BACK PEPLUM

IF NOT
THE SAME
ANGLE

FRONT PEPLUM

CF & CB
PARALLEL

12.

MATCH AT
SIDE SEAM/WAIST

CF & CB
PARALLEL

SPLIT THE
DIFFERENCE

13.

SAME
ANGLE

CF & CB
PARALLEL

Midriff Top w/ Peplum

TRUEING

FRONT PEPLUM

14.

- Using a straight ruler to straighten the following:
    - o CF/Center Front, Side Seam.
- SMOOTH the WAIST using the Vary Form Curve ruler. Make sure the line begins straight at the CF Waist but then slightly curves up toward the Side Seam.
- SMOOTH the HEM. You can use the Vary Form Curve ruler and/or a straight ruler; make sure the Hem is a smooth line and not "choppy".
- Make sure these corners are at a 90-degree angle:
    - o CF, at the Waist and Hem.
    - o Side Seam, at the Waist and Hem.

BACK PEPLUM

15.

- Using a straight ruler to straighten the following:
    - o CB/Center Back, Side Seam.
- SMOOTH the WAIST using the Vary Form Curve ruler. Make sure the line begins straight at the CB Waist but then slightly curves up toward the Side Seam.
- SMOOTH the HEM. You can use the Vary Form Curve ruler and/or a straight ruler; make sure the Hem is a smooth line and not "choppy".
- Make sure these corners are at a 90-degree angle:
    - o CB, at the Waist and Hem.
    - o Side Seam, at the Waist and Hem.

16.

- After Trueing the Peplum patterns, double check that the Side Seams are the same measurement and are on the same angle (following the BALANCING you did earlier).

17.

- Lastly, before adding Seam Allowances to the Peplum pattern pieces place both the FRONT and BACK Peplum pattern pieces together, matching them at the Side Seams...
- Check the WAIST and the HEM and make sure that when "joined" together at the Side Seams, that the WAIST and HEM lines are continuously SMOOTH; think about if you sewed the pattern pieces together, that when sewn, the WAIST and HEM would look like a nice smooth curve.

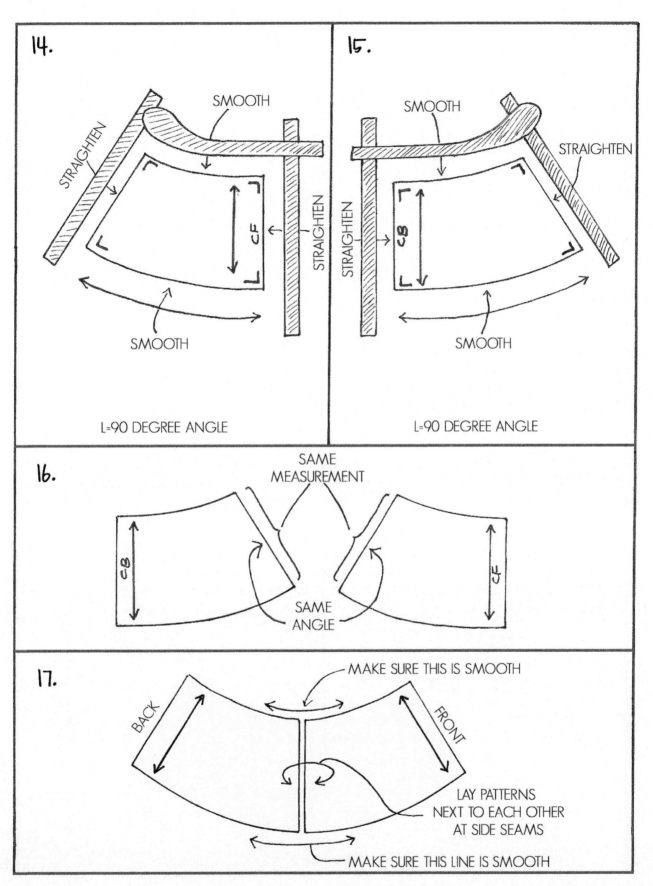

14.

STRAIGHTEN
SMOOTH
CF
SMOOTH
L=90 DEGREE ANGLE

15.

SMOOTH
STRAIGHTEN
STRAIGHTEN
CB
SMOOTH
L=90 DEGREE ANGLE

16.

SAME
MEASUREMENT
CB
CF
SAME
ANGLE

17.

MAKE SURE THIS IS SMOOTH
BACK
FRONT
LAY PATTERNS
NEXT TO EACH OTHER
AT SIDE SEAMS
MAKE SURE THIS LINE IS SMOOTH

Add Seam Allowances to the Waist Midriff with Peplum Top:

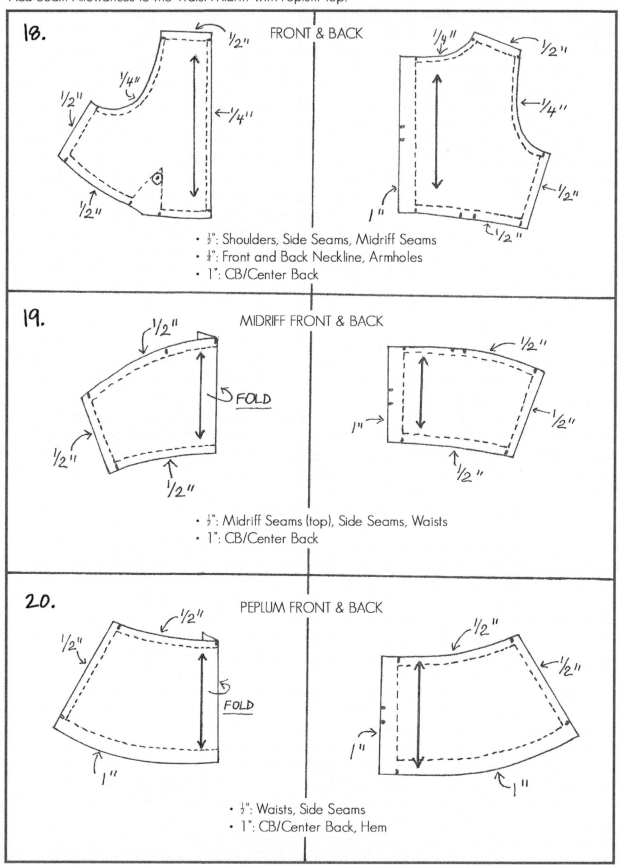

18. FRONT & BACK

½": Shoulders, Side Seams, Midriff Seams
- ¼": Front and Back Neckline, Armholes
- 1": CB/Center Back

19. MIDRIFF FRONT & BACK

- ½": Midriff Seams (top), Side Seams, Waists
- 1": CB/Center Back

20. PEPLUM FRONT & BACK

- ½": Waists, Side Seams
- 1": CB/Center Back, Hem

Midriff Top w/ Peplum

- After trueing waist midriff with peplum blouse and adding seam allowance, pin drape on the dress form. Make sure that the drape is pinned correctly based on the image below:

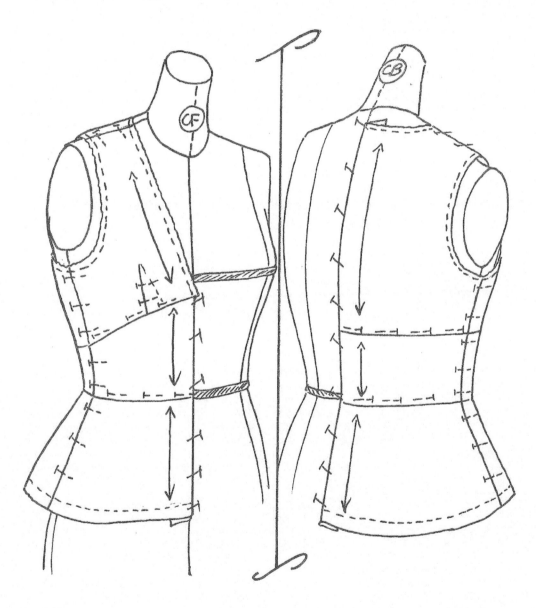

Midriff Top w/ Peplum

SEWING INSTRUCTIONS

- After draping midriff blouse with peplum and trueing the draped pieces onto dotted paper, cut out the pattern pieces with seam allowances using muslin and set aside to sew.

1. Sew darts in the front top sections. Remember when sewing darts, sew 1/2" past drill/punchhole. Press darts toward the front.

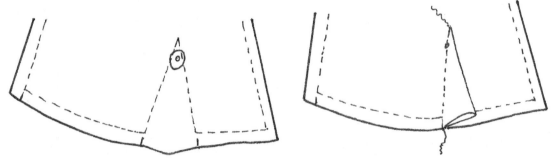

2. Sew shoulders. Take the front top sections and back top sections and attach both the right and left sides at 1/2" along the shoulders. Press seams open.

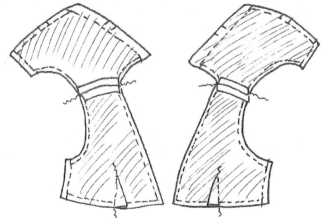

3. Press neckline edges 1/4" toward the wrong side of the garment (inside) and then edgestitch 1/8"

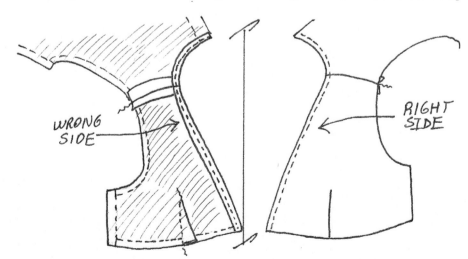

WRONG SIDE

RIGHT SIDE

87.

Midriff Top w/ Peplum

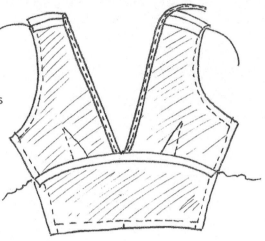

4. Sew the Front Top Sections to to Back Midriff at 1/2" seam allowance. Press seam allowances down toward the waist.

5. Sew Back Top Sections to Back Midriff at 1/2" seam allowance. Press seam allowances down toward the waist

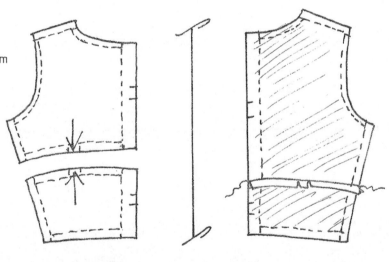

6. Sew Side Seams at 1/2" and press open

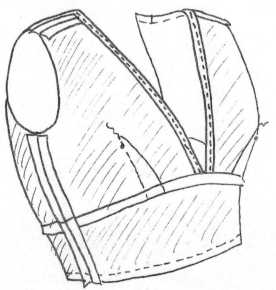

Midriff Top w/ Peplum

7. Turn under armhone edges 1/4" toward the wrong side (inside) and stitch 1/8" edgestitch. Press carefully, using steam to relieve some of the buckling and crimping that may occur in severe curves.

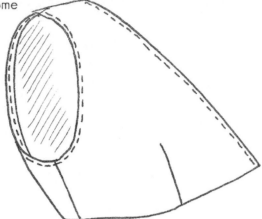

8. Sew the Peplum pieces, Front Peplum to Right Back Peplum and Left Back Peplum, at the side seams, using 1/2" seam allowance.

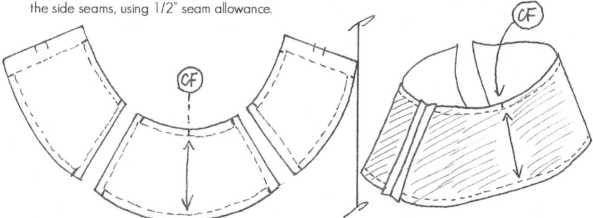

9. Attach sewn Top Section (at the waist) to the Peplum using 1/2" seam allowance, making sure the side seams match.

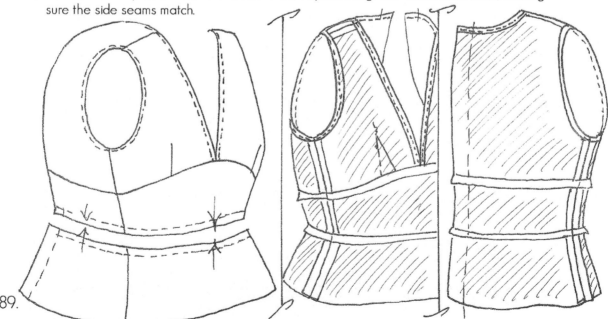

Midriff Top w/ Peplum

10. Sew Hem. Press the hem 1/2" under and sew 1/4" stitch. Do a final hem pressing.

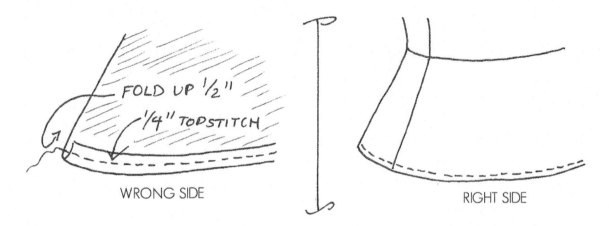

FOLD UP 1/2"

1/4" TOPSTITCH

WRONG SIDE

RIGHT SIDE

11. Place sewn garment on the dress to check the fit.

CIRCLE SKIRT

Circle Skirt

PREPARING THE MUSLIN

1. Prepping the fabric:
- In order to drape the CIRCLE SKIRT, you will need two (2) rectangular pieces of muslin, one for the FRONT and one for BACK skirt.
- Each will measure 42" X 42".
- Draw vertical (up and down) grainlines on each piece of muslin, 1" away from one of the edges/sides.

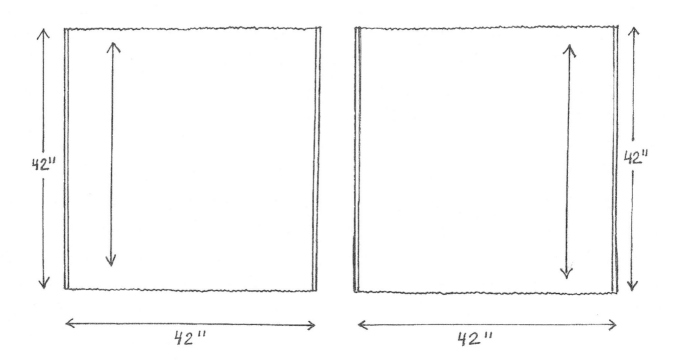

Circle Skirt

PREPARING THE MUSLIN

2. Mark the fabric:
  • Before you mark the fabric, press under and fold the sides that you marked with the 1" grainline

FRONT SKIRT MUSLIN PIECE:
  • Measure 5" down from the top edge of the fabric on the 1" folded grainline and mark. This will be the CF Waist, label "CF" or "CF Waist".
  • From the 5" mark, measure 7" down and draw a perfect front crossgrain line at this level. You can use your L-square to make sure this line is perpendicular.
  • This is the HIP level of the skirt.

BACK SKIRT MUSLIN PIECE:
  • On the folded 1" grainline edge of the BACK skirt muslin piece, measure 12" down from the top edge.
  • Draw a perfect back crossgrain line at this level. You can use your L-square to make sure this line is perpendicular.
  • This is the HIP level of the skirt.

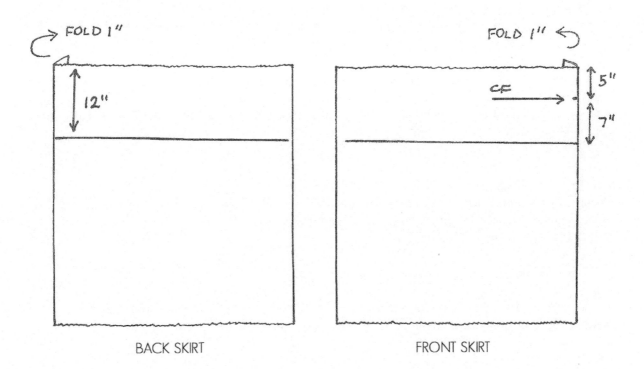

BACK SKIRT   FRONT SKIRT

Circle Skirt
FRONT DRAPE

1. Pin the CF grainline (that is pressed/folded under) at the CF of the Dress Form.
- When pinning, make sure that you pin the 5" CF WAIST mark on the CF Waist position of the Dress Form.
- Then, make sure to pin the 7" mark as shown.
- Continue pinning down the CF of the Dress Form.
- On the HIP LINE mark (7" level), smooth toward the Princess Seam of the Dress Form and pin.

2. Drape the front waistline to the Princess Seam.
- Smooth fabric toward the Princess Seam, at the WAIST and pin.
- Clip the fabric from the top edge to the WAIST and place a pin at the Princess Seam.

3. Drape the first flare of the Circle Skirt.
- Pivot the fabric downward from the waistline at the Princess Seam, and you will begin to see a flare being created right at that Princess Seam area.
- You will also see the crossgrain line begin to shift downward as well.

4. Draping the next Flares of the Circle Skirt.
- At the WAIST, keep clipping and pinning, pivoting the fabric downward until a second flare is created next to the first one.
- This second flare will create itself around the mid-hip area/center of the Side Front Princess Panel area of the Dress Form.

5. Finish the Front Drape.
- Keep clipping and pinning at the waist until you get the desired flares for the front of your Circle Skirt.
- Once you are satisfied, pin at the SIDE SEAM/WAIST position.
- Mark the skirt drape at these positions:
    - o Waist
    - o Side Seam
    - o Hem
- For the Hem, let the muslin fabric fall naturally, and then mark the desired Hem of your Circle Skirt by drawing lines that are parallel to the floor, or parallel to the bottom of the Dress Form.

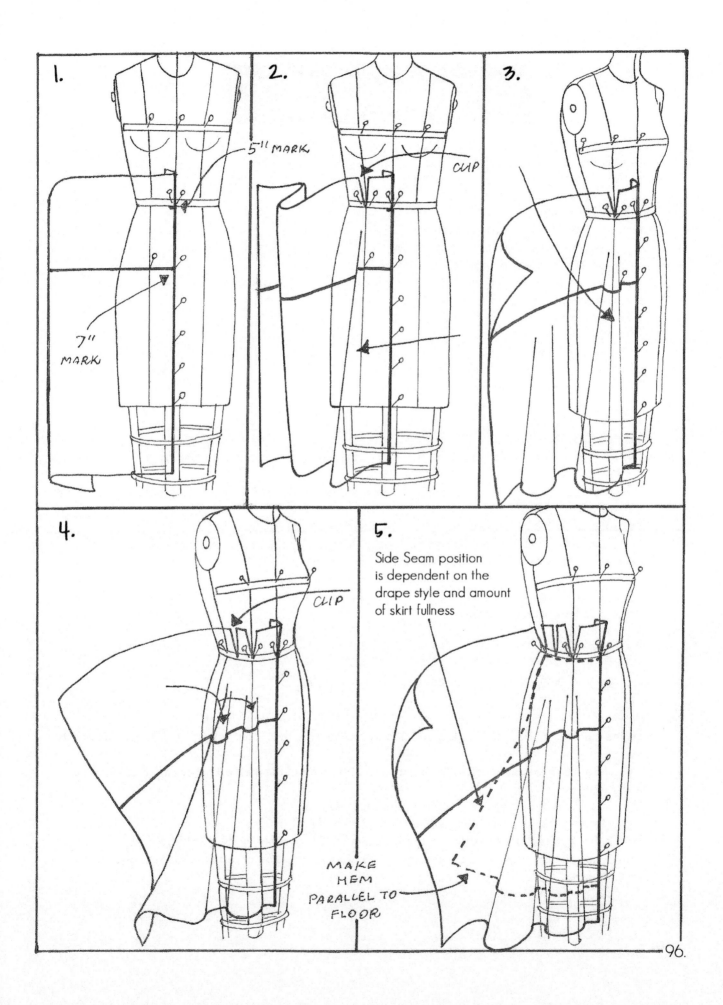

1.

5" MARK

7" MARK

2.

CLIP

3.

4.

CLIP

5.

Side Seam position is dependent on the drape style and amount of skirt fullness

MAKE HEM PARALLEL TO FLOOR

Circle Skirt

TRUEING THE DRAPE & CUTTING THE BACK

6. Trueing the Front Skirt Drape.
- First "true" the FRONT SKIRT drape, making sure:
    - o The waistline is smooth and not choppy
    - o The side seam line is straight
    - o The hem line starts out straight and perpendicular at the CF and SIDE HEM but is curved and smooth for the rest of the hem.
- Add seam allowances to the drape:
    - o Waist: $\frac{1}{2}$"
    - o Side Seam: $\frac{1}{2}$"
    - o Hem: 1"- 1 $\frac{1}{2}$"
- Cut excess muslin up to the seam allowance line.

7. Cutting the Back Skirt Drape.
- You will use the FRONT skirt to cut the BACK, so essentially you only have to DRAPE the FRONT and not the BACK:
- Take the other 42" X 42" cut muslin, that was going to be for the BACK Circle Skirt, and lay that on the pattern/cutting table.
- Place the FRONT skirt drape on top of the 42" X 42" muslin fabric.
- Match the crossgrains of the front and back skirts. At the same time, place the centerfold grainlines parallel, meaning the FRONT and BACK are parallel to one another.
- Allow the FRONT cut skirt drape to extend $\frac{1}{2}$" over the BACK muslin piece.
- Once you have properly positioned the FRONT on top of the BACK muslin piece (as shown in image), "trace" the front skirt lines at the
    - o Waist
    - o Side Seam
    - o Hem
- Cut excess muslin from that second 42" X 42" piece of muslin.

8. Place your drape on the Dress Form to readjust BACK WAIST position and check FIT.
- Pin the Front to the Back Skirt at the Side Seams, making sure that you are using the $\frac{1}{2}$" seam allowance line.
- If you have cut and pinned correctly, the front and back crossgrain lines will match at the Side Seams (see image).
- Place the Circle Skirt Drape and pin on to the Dress Form at CF.
- Go to the BACK and readjust the position of the BACK WAIST by dropping it $\frac{1}{2}$" at CB. This will allow for a better fit (traditionally the CB waist position is 1/2 " lower than the CF waist position).
- Lastly, check the FIT of your drape, making sure the Circle Skirt is balanced and has enough flare for your approval.

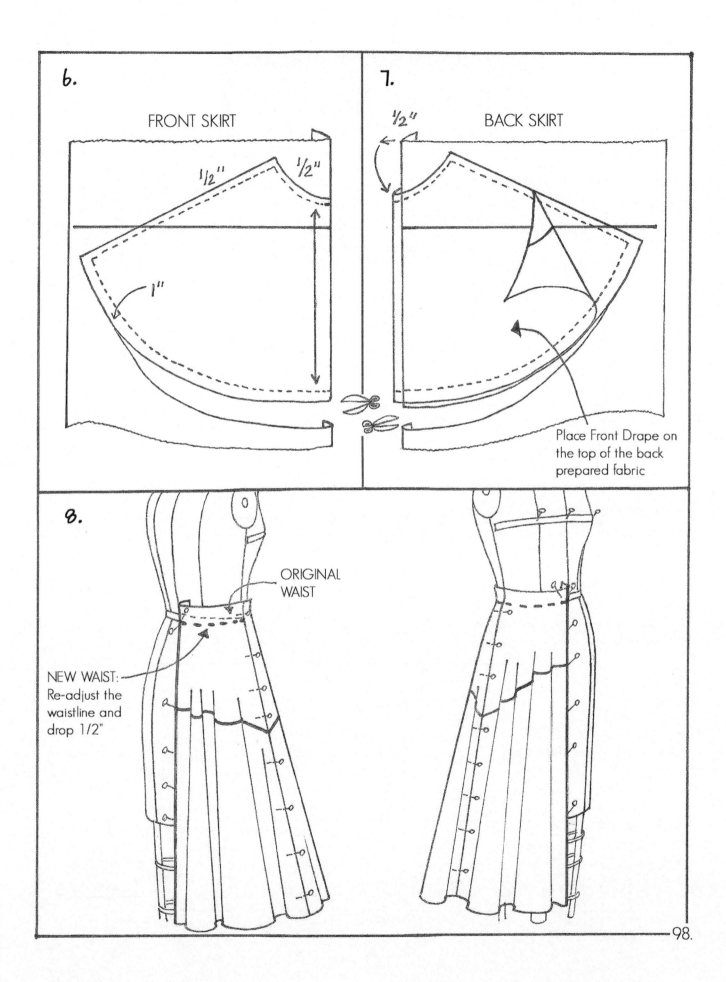

6.

FRONT SKIRT

$^1/_2$"

$^1/_2$"

1"

7.

$^1/_2$"

BACK SKIRT

Place Front Drape on
the top of the back
prepared fabric

8.

ORIGINAL
WAIST

NEW WAIST:
Re-adjust the
waistline and
drop 1/2"

Circle Skirt

DRAFTING A WAISTBAND

• This basic waistband is based on a style of waistband that opens in the back.

  Measurements needed:
  • Waist measurement + $\frac{1}{2}$" ease
  • Example here: 27" + $\frac{1}{2}$" = 27 $\frac{1}{2}$" total
  • Front Measurement: 14"
  • Back Measurement: 13 $\frac{1}{2}$" total; therefore, the RT BACK and LT BACK will each be 6 $\frac{3}{4}$"
  • Width of Finished Waistband: Here, the FINISHED WIDTH is 1 $\frac{1}{4}$"

1. Cut a rectangle that is 27 $\frac{1}{2}$" long and 2 $\frac{1}{2}$" wide (DOUBLE the finished width)

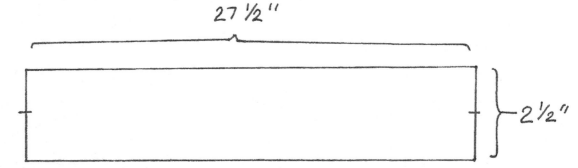

27 ½ "

2½"

2. Add a 1" extension (for closures like buttons, hook & eyes) onto one end of the pattern piece so now the length will be 28 $\frac{1}{2}$" long.
  • Make sure to mark where the 1" extension begins with NOTCHES.

1" EXTENSION

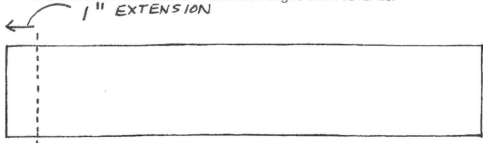

3. Divide the waistband pattern piece so you mark:
  • Center Front "CF", Side Seams "SS", Center Back "CB".
  • Mark these locations with NOTCHES.

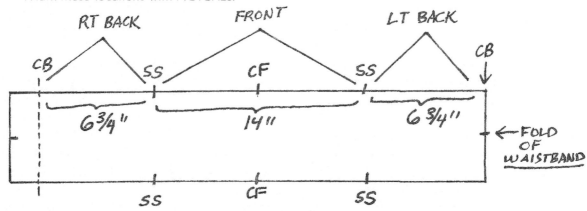

RT BACK   FRONT   LT BACK

CB   SS   CF   SS   CB

6¾"   14"   6¾"

FOLD OF WAISTBAND

SS   CF   SS

99.

Circle Skirt
SEWING INSTRUCTIONS

• After draping the Circle Skirt and trueing the draped pieces onto dotted paper, cut the pattern pieces with seam allowances in muslin. Set them aside to sew.

1. Draft waistband with extension, including the interfacing pattern:
  • After cutting the waistband in muslin, cut fusible interfacing as well, which is half the full waistband pattern piece plus 1/2" extra.
  • Iron on the fusible interfacing to the waistband.

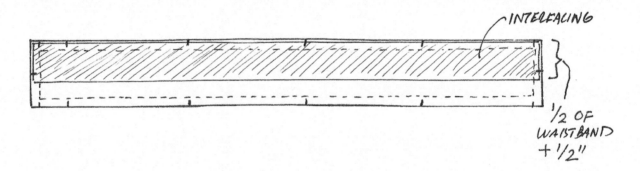

INTERFACING

} 1/2 OF WAISTBAND + 1/2"

2. Sew the Circle Skirt:
  • Sew the side seams at 1/2" seam allowances. Press open.

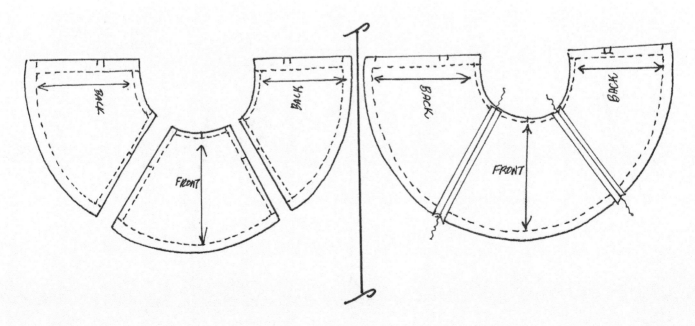

BACK   BACK   FRONT

BACK   BACK   FRONT

Circle Skirt

SEWING INSTRUCTIONS

3. Sew Center Back seams, at 1" seam allowance. Sew up to zipper notches. Press Open.

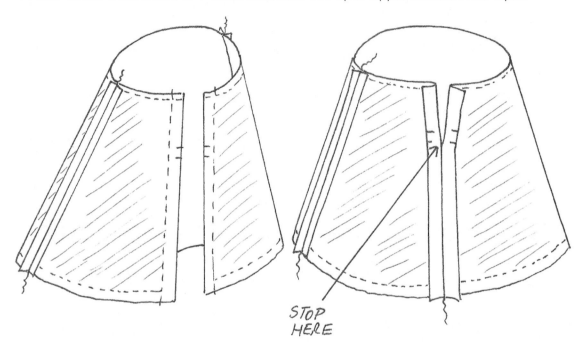

STOP HERE

4. Sew a 7" zipper at the CB. Reminder: You still need to sew the waistband onto the top of the skirt, therefore, make sure to leave 1/2" seam allowance above the top of the zipper to sew to the waistband.

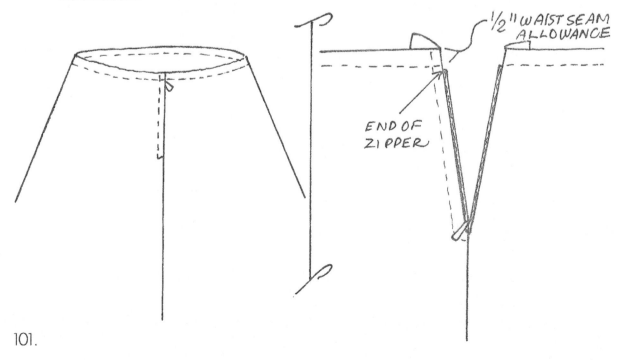

1/2" WAIST SEAM ALLOWANCE

END OF ZIPPER

Circle Skirt

SEWING INSTRUCTIONS

5. Fold the WAISTBAND in half lengthwise, correct sides together...
- Stitch one end of the waistband closed and stitch the extension end closed as shown, using the appropriate seam allowance – normally it is $\frac{1}{4}$" or $\frac{1}{2}$".
- You can trim/cut the corners and edges to allow for sharper edges once you turn the waistband to its right side.

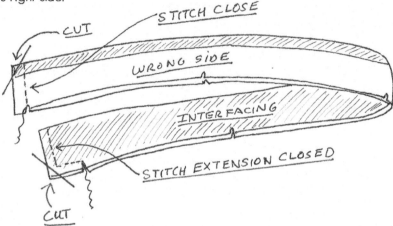

6. Turn the WAISTBAND correct side out and press:

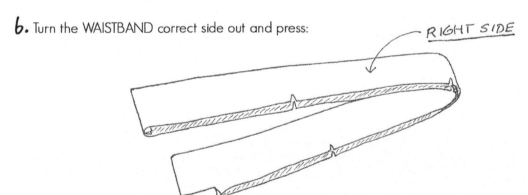

7. With the correct side of the SKIRT facing you, pin the interfaced side of the WAISTBAND - one layer only - to the correct side of the SKIRT:

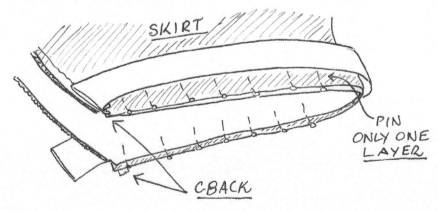

Circle Skirt

SEWING INSTRUCTIONS

8. Stitch the pinned one layer of the WAISTBAND to the SKIRT, sewng at ½" seam allowance:

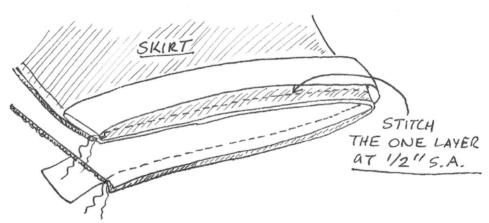

9. Turn the WAISTBAND to the correct side of the SKIRT...
  • Pin the UNSEWN layer of the WAISTBAND over the stitchline, making sure to sandwich the seam allowance inside the waistband.

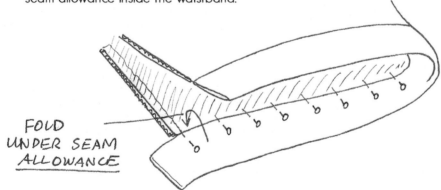

10. From the outside of the skirt, edge stitch along the edge of the waistband:

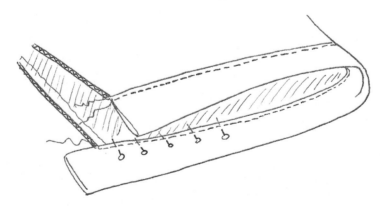

Circle Skirt

SEWING INSTRUCTIONS

11. Sew the waistband to the skirt. The 1" Tab Extension should be on the LEFT of the Back Skirt

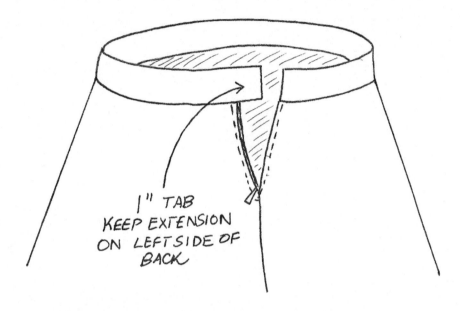

1" TAB
KEEP EXTENSION
ON LEFT SIDE OF
BACK

12. Sew the hem of the Circle Skirt. The Circle Skirt has a 1" hem. There are several ways to hem a Circle Skirt. Below are two methods:

• Press the hem after sewing.

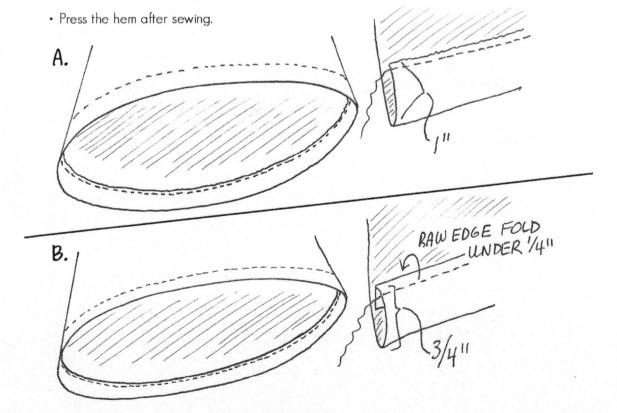

A.

1"

B.

RAW EDGE FOLD
UNDER 1/4"

3/4"

Circle Skirt

SEWING INSTRUCTIONS

• 3 Additional Hem Options:

C. 1/2" Raw edge hem

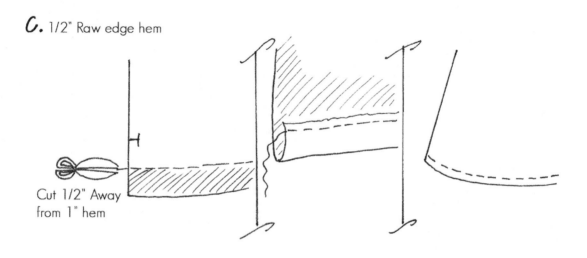

Cut 1/2" Away
from 1" hem

D. 1/4" Top stitch hem

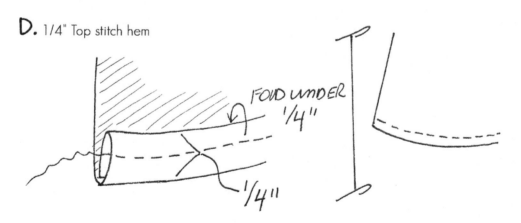

FOLD UNDER 1/4"

1/4"

E. Bias tape covered hem

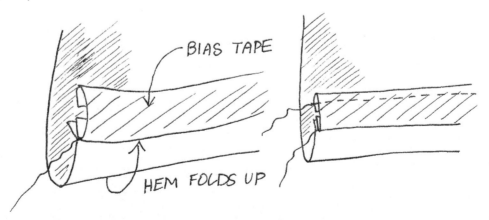

BIAS TAPE

HEM FOLDS UP

COWL TOP

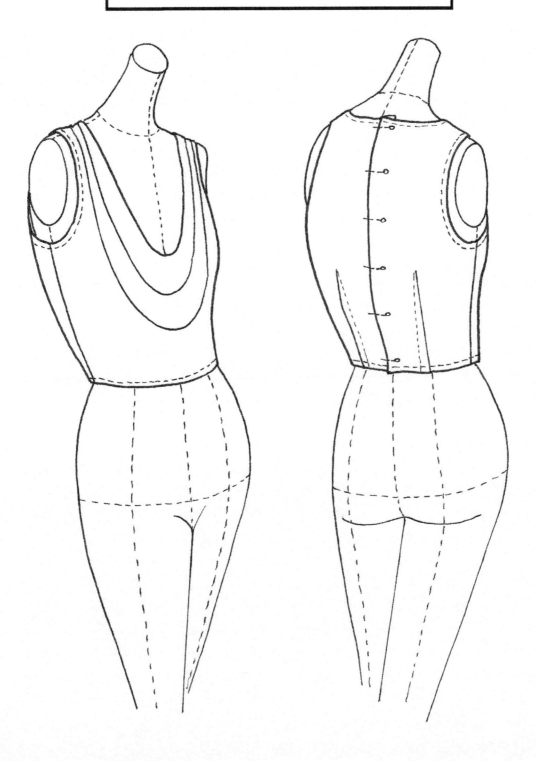

Cowl Top

BIAS COWL NECK TOP OR TUNIC

A. Bias Cowl Neck Top: Front and Back--WITHOUT pleats at shoulder or WITH pleats at shoulder.

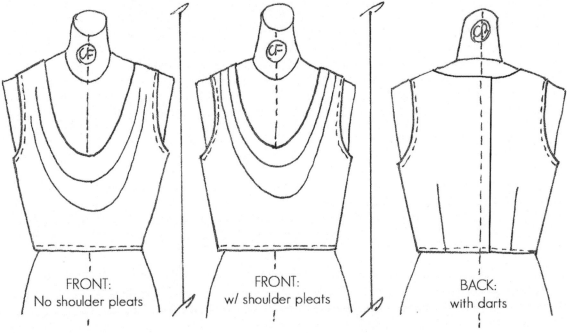

FRONT:
No shoulder pleats

FRONT:
w/ shoulder pleats

BACK:
with darts

B. Bias Cowl Neck Tunic: Front and Back--The Back can be done in two (2) ways:
Bias-cut or on the Straight Grain with fisheye darts at waist.

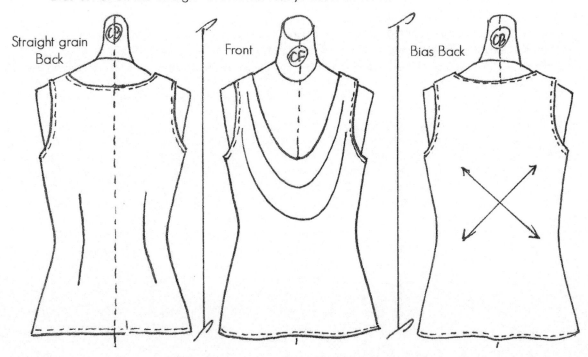

Straight grain
Back

Front

Bias Back

Cowl Top

PREPARING THE MUSLIN

1. Cutting the fabric: For the Cowl Drape, it is preferable to use lighter/softer fabric, such as a lighter-weight muslin or light-weight satin (like georgette, charmeuse).
- For this Cowl Drape, this cut-piece of fabric will be used to drape the FRONT.
- Measure and cut a perfect square 34" X 34".
- Draw a TRUE BIAS line diagonally across the piece of fabric. To find the true bias, you can draw a small perfect square in the middle of the fabric and draw a diagonal line across the square. Extend that line from one corner of the 34" X 34" square cut piece of fabric to the other corner.

2. Fold the NECKLINE and SELF-FACING AREA:
- Determine the NECKLINE edge and self-facing area on the cut fabric. This is typically on the TOP RIGHT of the 34" X 34" cut square piece of fabric.
- Fold the corner enough so the folded area measures to about 21" long, as shown in the image. This should give you enough length to drape the cowl neckline of the top.

3. Cutting and Marking the BACK pieces. The Back pieces for this Top will NOT be on the BIAS.
- Cut one piece of fabric (lighter-weight muslin) measuring 23" Long X 12" Wide.
- Draw a vertical (up-and-down) CB grainline 1" away from the left side edge.
- Press that 1" area under so it is folded.
- From the top edge of the cut fabric, measure 3" down and mark. This is the CB Neck.
- From the 3" mark, measure $4\frac{1}{4}$" down and mark. This is the "across back/shoulder blade" level.
- At this $4\frac{1}{4}$" level, draw a crossgrain line across the fabric. You can use the L-square to make sure that line is perfectly squared and horizontal.
- From the folded edge, on that crossgrain line, measure about 7" in towards the cut fabric, and draw a crossmark. This position will be the Armplate Crossmark.
- You are finished prepping the BACK fabric pieces. Set these aside for when it is time to drape the BACK of the Cowl Top.

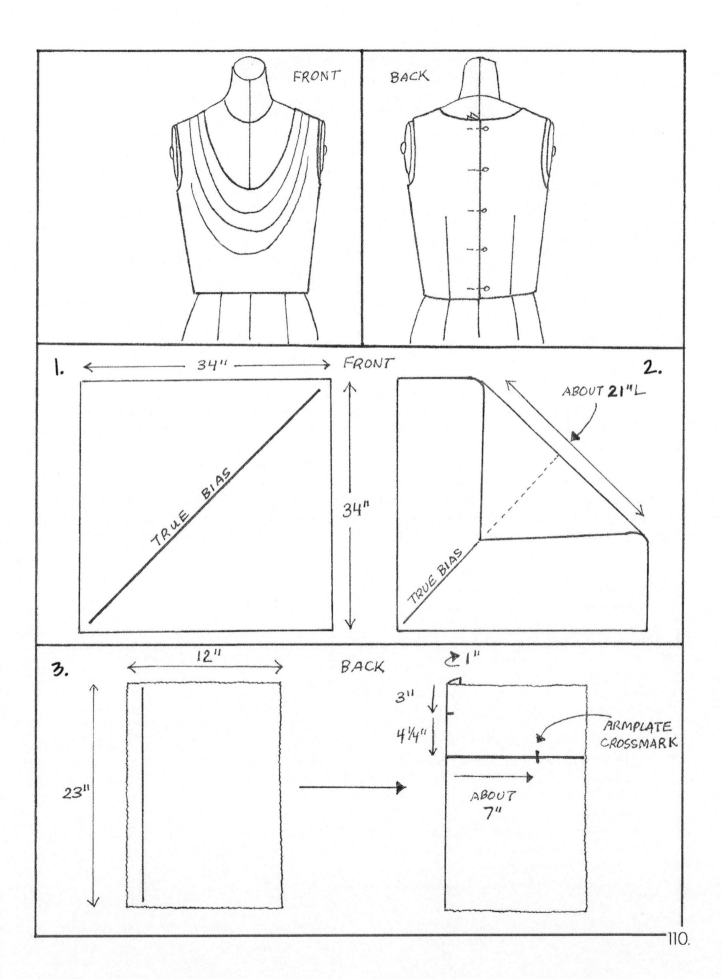

FRONT   BACK

1.
← —— 34" —— →   FRONT

TRUE BIAS

↕ 34"

2.
ABOUT **21"**L

TRUE BIAS

3.
← —— 12" —— →   BACK

↕ 23"

↺ 1"

3" ↓

4¼" ↓

ARMPLATE
CROSSMARK

ABOUT
7" →

Cowl Top

FRONT DRAPE W/ PLEATS

1. Prepare the Dress Form:
   - Determine the desired neckline depth: How deep the cowl neckline will go. Place a pin at that position on the CF of the Dress Form.
   - Next, place pins on each shoulder at the position where you want the neckline edge to be on the SHOULDERS.

2. Begin draping:
   - Place the folded edge of the fabric on top of the Dress Form as shown, making sure the TRUE BIAS line is at the CF of the Dress Form.
   - Make sure the middle of the folded edge is placed where you placed the pin at the CF of the Dress Form. The folded edge will be folded under and therefore act as a SELF FACING for the Cowl Top.

3. Drape the Cowl Drape:
   - Drape the center front cowl neckline by placing the folded edge of the fabric up and onto the shoulders of the Dress Form.
   - Place pins on the shoulder as you drape the cowl. Try to do this evenly by doing one shoulder first...then the other...all the while MAKING SURE that the CF bias line stays straight at the CF.
   - As you drape the cowl, and pin the shoulder, you can go back to the CF and pin the drape/fabric at the CF so it doesn't shift.
   - If you want additional cowl drapes, lift and PLEAT each shoulder to form additional cowl drapes (see image), all the while still making sure the BIAS grain stays straight up and down on the CF of the Dress Form.

4. Trimming and Clipping the Cowl Drape:
   - Trim and clip the WAISTLINE, cutting out the excess fabric, to allow for a smoothly draped waist.
   - Pin the WAIST.
   - Smooth the WAIST and sides and pin into place at the SIDE SEAM.
   - Clip to ease the smoothing and trim off excess fabric on the sides as well.

5. Mark the Cowl Front Drape:
   - Mark the following on the draped fabric:
     o Shoulder Seam
     o Side Seam
     o Waistline
     o Armhole area-Crossmark 1" below:
        - armplate
        - middle of armplate
        - shoulder crossmarks at the folded pleats (if there are pleats)

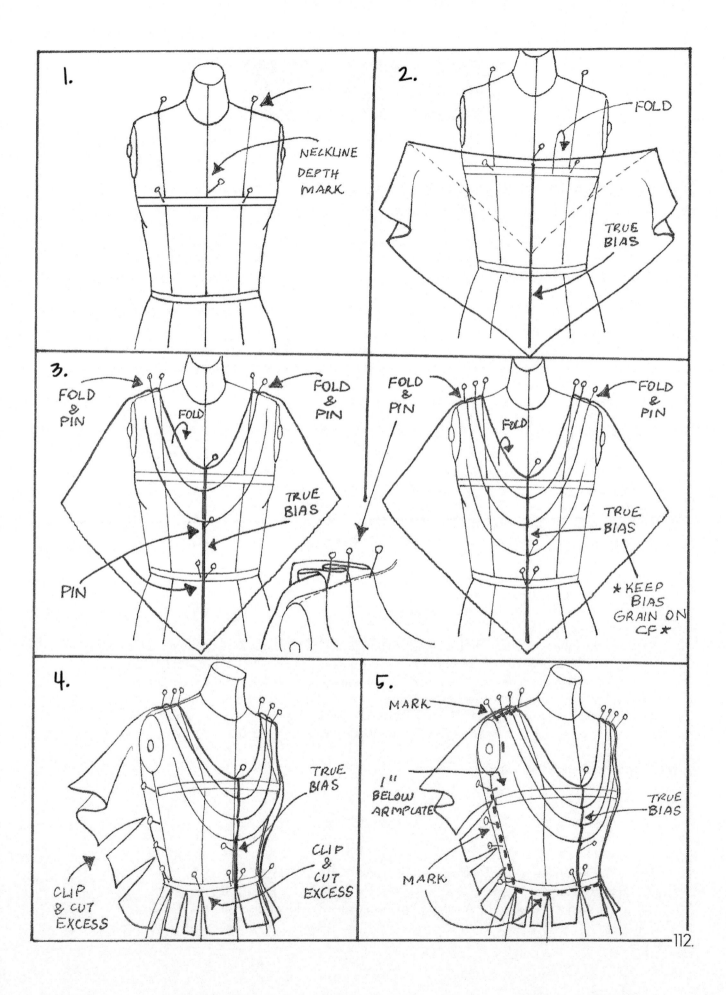

1. NECKLINE DEPTH MARK

2. FOLD / TRUE BIAS

3. FOLD & PIN / FOLD / FOLD & PIN / TRUE BIAS / PIN / FOLD & PIN / FOLD / FOLD & PIN / TRUE BIAS / *KEEP BIAS GRAIN ON CF*

4. TRUE BIAS / CLIP & CUT EXCESS / CLIP & CUT EXCESS

5. MARK / 1" BELOW ARMPLATE / MARK / TRUE BIAS

112.

Cowl Top

BACK DRAPE W/ DARTS

1. Place cut fabric piece and line up the CB folded side to the CB of the Dress Form:
- Place the 3" mark at the CB NECK position of the Dress Form, pin in place.
- Follow this by pinning the 4 ¼" mark on the CB of the Dress Form.
- Pin the rest of the fabric at the CB of the Dress Form, as shown, down to the WAIST.
- Pin the crossgrain line at the SHOULDER BLADE level down to the ARMPLATE. Make sure this line is parallel to the bottom of the Dress Form and not shifting up or down. Pin to the 7" mark at the armplate edge.

2. Draw the WAIST DART:
- At the WAIST level, smooth the fabric to the Princess Seam, draw a short mark at the WAIST.
- Measure 1 ¼" away from that first mark (towards the side seam), and draw another short mark.
- Now measure 7" up toward the shoulder, on the Princess Seam and mark. You can lightly draw a dart, as shown, to help you with the folding of this dart.

3. Fold and Pin the Dart.
- Take the FIRST mark you made on the fabric at the Princess Seam/Waist and folded over to touch the SECOND mark 1 ¼" away. By doing this, you have draped the WAIST DART. Pin the dart down as shown so it is secured.

4. Clip the WAIST, NECK and smooth the SIDE SEAM:
- After you finish folding and pinning the WAIST DART, smooth, clip, and pin the WAIST.
- Smooth the fabric past the SIDE SEAM, and pin fabric into place.
- Go back up to the NECK area. Clip, and pin the NECK to the SHOULDER.
- Trim excess fabric away, as shown.

5. Drop the Neckline:
- Unpin the fabric from the CB NECK position and re-pin fabric about 2" down from the CB NECK, at center back. This will be your neck CB NECK position. Because the front cowl drape is so open, the CB neck position needs to be dropped so it is in harmony with the rest of the neckline.
- Clip and pin from this new position, up to the SHOULDER position, as shown in image.
- Once you have pinned at the SHOULDER position, smooth fabric past the shoulder.
- Trim any excess fabric from side seam, waist, shoulder and/or neck area.

6. Drape the Shoulder and Mark the Drape:
- Pin the shoulder area down.
- Mark the following:
  - Neckline
  - Shoulder
  - Waist
  - Waist Dart (re-mark the folded positions as well as top of dart)
  - Side Seam
  - Crossmark: 1" below the Armplate, Mid-Armplate, Shoulder edge

113.

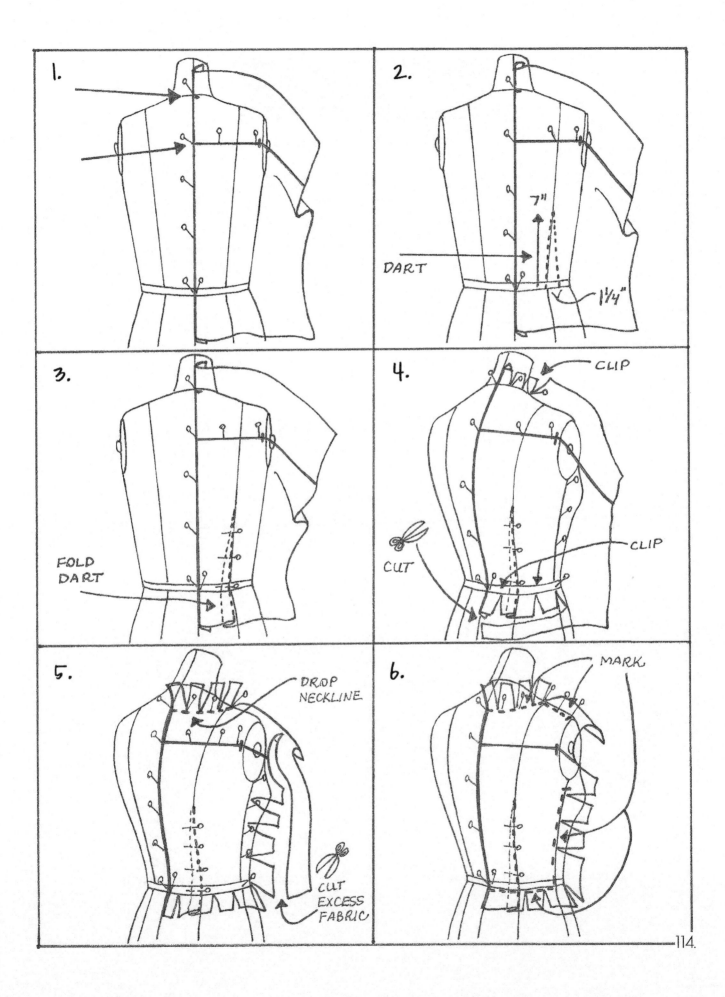

1.

2.

DART

7"

1¼"

3.

FOLD
DART

4.

CLIP

CLIP

CUT

5.

DROP
NECKLINE

CUT
EXCESS
FABRIC

6.

MARK

Cowl Top

SEWING INSTRUCTIONS

1. Sew Darts to back pieces first. Press the darts toward Center Back (CB) and set aside.

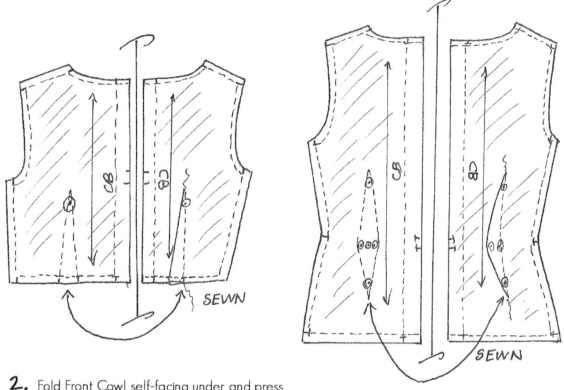

SEWN

SEWN

2. Fold Front Cowl self-facing under and press.

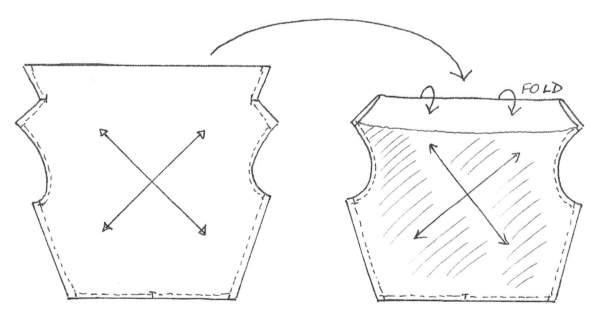

FOLD

3. Sew a basting stitch at 3/8" right next to the 1/2" seam allowance to keep front self-facing down. This stitch can be removed after the top is finished?

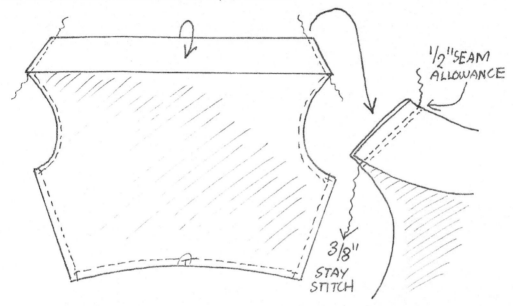

1/2" SEAM ALLOWANCE

3/8" STAY STITCH

4. Sew the Side Seams by sewing the Front Cowl Top to Back Top at 1/2" seam allowance. Press Open.

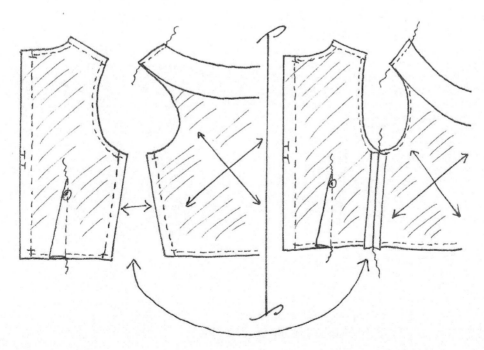

Cowl Top

SEWING INSTRUCTIONS

5. Sew shoulder of Cowl Top at 1/2" seam allowance. Press open.

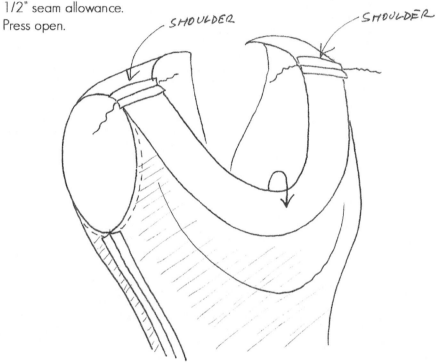

6. Clean finish the armholes. Fold armhole edges 1/4" and edgestitch. Press. Do the same for the back neckline.

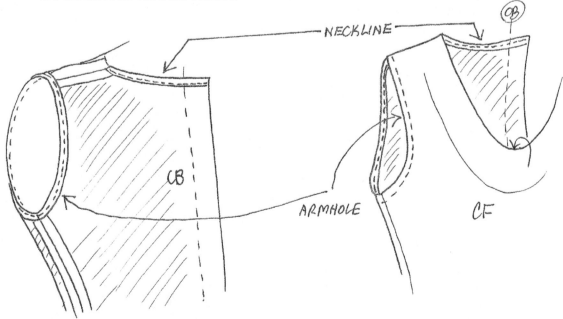

Cowl Top
SEWING INSTRUCTIONS

7. Sew hem. Fold the bottom of the Bias Cowl Top 1/2" and press. Sew a 1/4" topstitch. Press again.

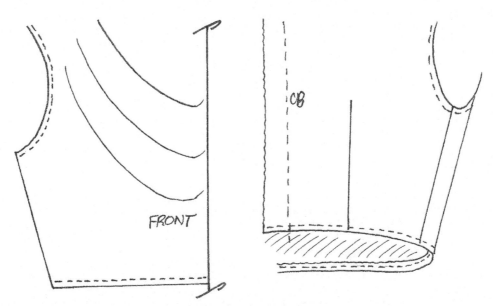

FRONT

CB

8. Do a final pressing and put on the dress form to check the fit.

CF

CB

BIAS SLIP DRESS

Bias Slip Dress

PREPARING THE FABRIC

- Cut 2 pieces of muslin (Front & Back), both 45" x 45".

- Draw a TRUE BIAS line diagonally across the piece of fabric. To find the true bias, you can draw a small perfect square in the middle of the fabric and draw a diagonal line across the square. Extend that line from one corner of the 45" X 45" square cut piece of fabric to the other corner.

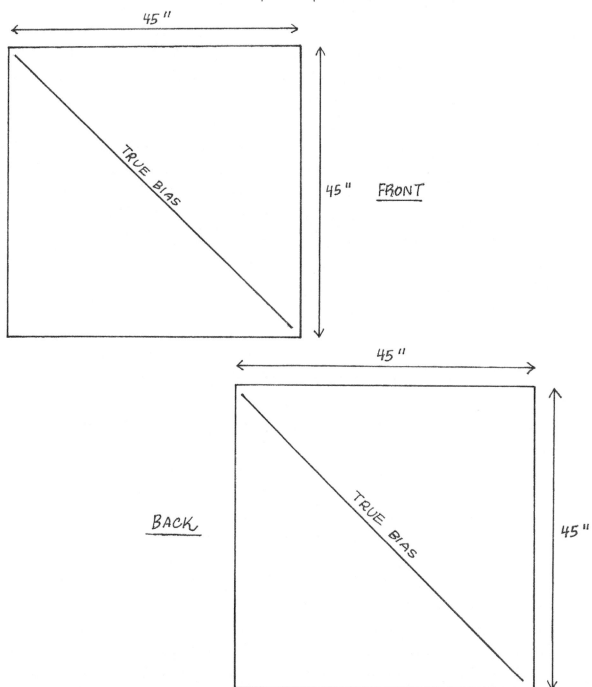

Bias Slip Dress

Preparing the Dress Form

- For the traditional Bias Slip Dress Style, place PINS or STYLE TAPE on the neckline of the Dress Form.
- Make sure to mark the:
  - o Front Neckline-This can be "V"-shape (as shown) or scooped
  - o Straps
  - o Back Neckline

USE

DRAPING TAPE

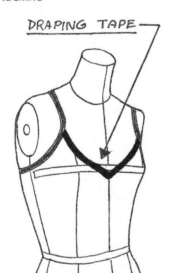

OR

PINS

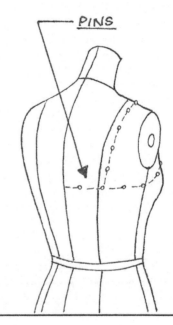

Example of a V-Neck
Bias Slip Dress:

FRONT

BACK

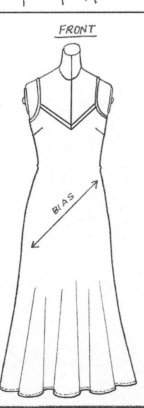

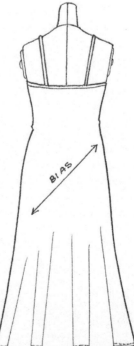

BIAS

BIAS

Bias Slip Dress

FRONT DRAPE

1. Take one of the 45" X 45" cut pieces of fabric and pin the bias line of the fabric to the CF of the Dress Form.
  - When placing the fabric on the Dress Form, make sure the top corner/point of the cut fabric reaches the top of the Dress Form level.

2. Smooth, Clip, and Drape: Because the fabric is on the BIAS, you will notice that it "stretches" and hugs the body. As a result, many people feel the need to smooth the fabric very tightly; DO NOT DO THIS! Let the fabric and bias of the fabric MOLD over the body; DO NOT PULL, but SMOOTH.
  - Smooth, clip and pin the fabric across the NECKLINE style line. About 2" from the CF, clip the fabric from the top edge to the NECKLINE styleline. Pin the NECKLINE.
  - Next, carefully smooth the fabric toward the SIDE SEAM and Upper Torso/Bust area.

3. Side Bust Dart or No Bust Dart:
  - Dart: Although the fabric is on the bias (and therefore "stretches") and depending on the weight of the fabric used, you might still find the need to drape a BUST DART for a better fit around the bust area. If so, fold a small dart about 1 ½"-2" below the underarm edge of the NECKLINE.

  - No Dart: If you are using very thin, chiffon-like fabric, you might be able to drape the Bias Slip Dress around the bust area with no need for a BUST DART. If so, carefully smooth the fabric towards the bust/side seam area and pin at the side seam (see image).

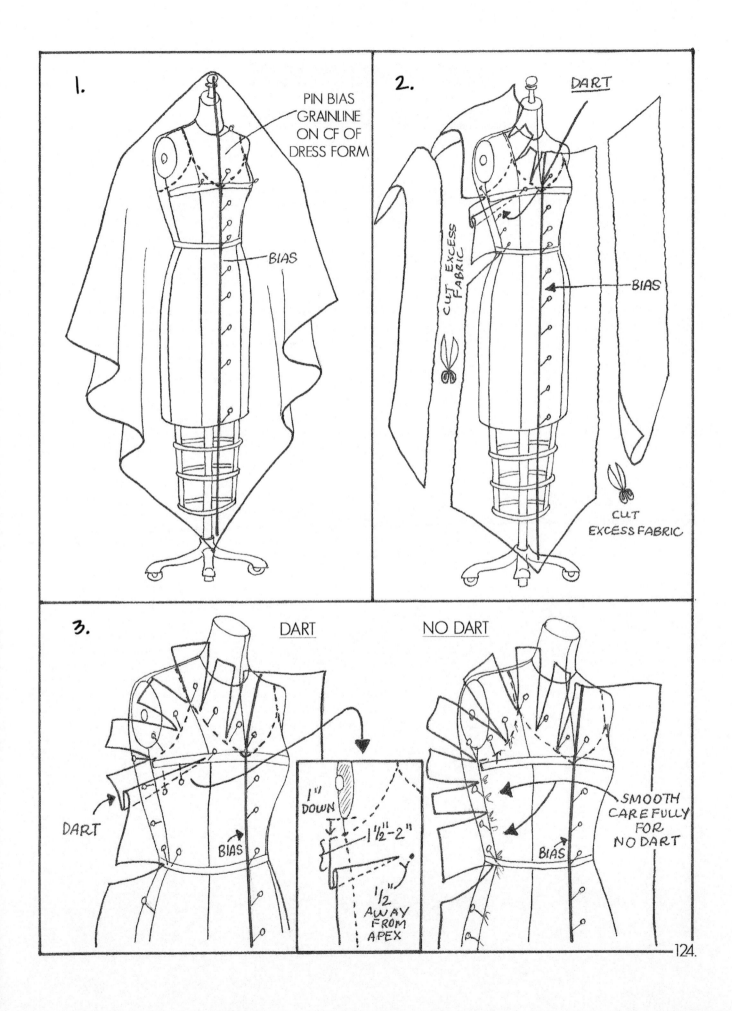

1.

PIN BIAS
GRAINLINE
ON CF OF
DRESS FORM

BIAS

2.

DART

CUT EXCESS FABRIC

BIAS

CUT
EXCESS FABRIC

3.

DART

NO DART

DART

BIAS

1" DOWN

1½"-2"

½" AWAY FROM APEX

SMOOTH
CAREFULLY
FOR
NO DART

BIAS

Bias Slip Dress

FRONT DRAPE

4. Continue Draping the Bias Slip Dress.
  - After draping the DART (if needed), smooth fabric slightly toward the side seam to about WAIST level.
  - As you drape the rest of the Dress, create a slight flowing flare/flutter at the Princess Seam area, from the high hip down. This flare/flutter is a trait of a Bias Dress, adding slight sweep of the dress.
  - You can create a small flutter or larger one, depending on how much sweep/swing you prefer for the Bias Dress silhouette.
  - Once you are satisfied with the bias flare/flutter in the middle of one side of the Dress Form, smooth and clip at the SIDE SEAM, WAIST area, and pin at the WAIST, as well as the rest of the SIDE SEAM.

5. Marking the FRONT Bias Dress Drape.
  - Mark all the key areas of the Dress Form on the Front Drape:
      o Front Bustline/Neckline
      o Waistline: Draw a small crossmark at the Waist level
      o Side Seam
      o Hem: Follow the bottom of the Dress Form, making sure it is parallel to the floor.

Keep FRONT DRAPE on the Dress Form so when you drape the BACK, you can pin it to the BACK Drape, at the side seams for final drape fit check.

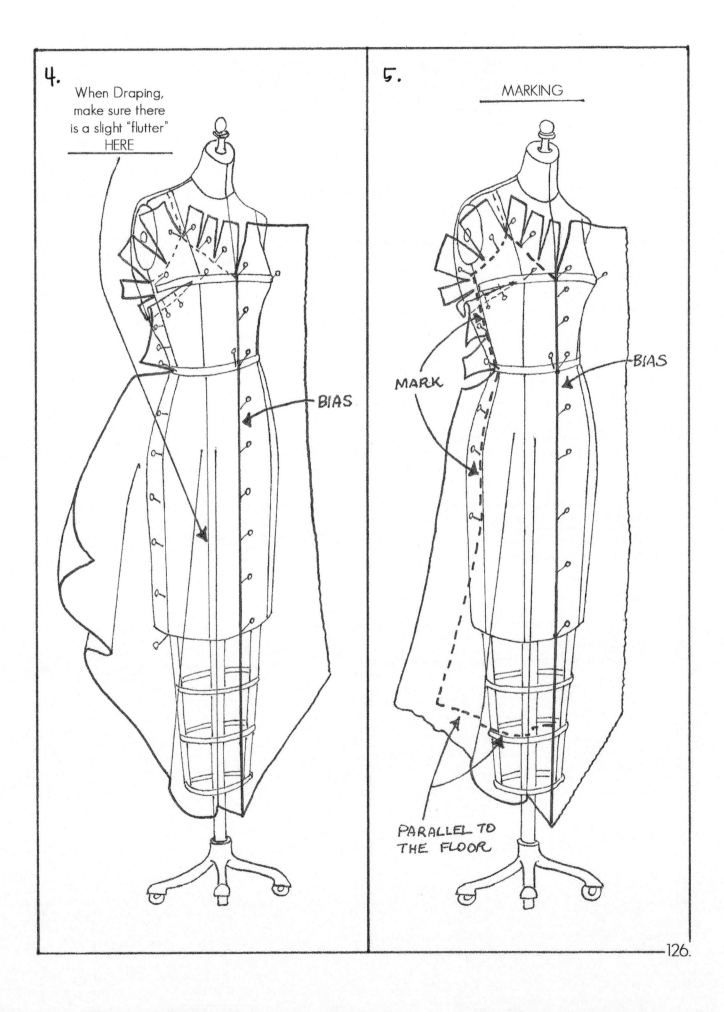

4.

When Draping,
make sure there
is a slight "flutter"
HERE

BIAS

5.

MARKING

MARK

BIAS

PARALLEL TO
THE FLOOR

Bias Slip Dress

BACK DRAPE

1. Pin the Bias line of the fabric to the CB position of the Dress Form.
- When beginning to pin, make sure the top "point"/corner of the fabric hits the top of the Dress Form, around the NECK area, as shown.
- Pin the fabric down the CB of the dress form, making sure it is secure and will not shift. It is recommended to pin at 1"-1 ½" intervals to make sure the fabric is secure.

2. Smooth, Drape, and Clip.
- Remember to SMOOTH not PULL, when draping the bias fabric.
- Begin smoothing the fabric toward the SIDE SEAM, at the upper torso area following the back bustline styleline that you had previously marked (either with style tape or pins). Pin at the SIDE SEAM to WAIST level. Clip to help ease the draping process.
- As you are draping and smoothing, begin to create "flutters"/flares, similar to the ones created for the FRONT Bias Slip Dress Drape. These flares usually are formed naturally as you drape, beginning from the waist and high-hip area.
- Look at the flutters/flares that you created in the FRONT drape, so the BACK drapes match it equally, with the same amount of flares.
- Once you are satisfied with the flares and drape of the back slip dress, smooth the fabric towards the SIDE SEAM and pin.

3. Mark the BACK Drape:
- After you are satisfied with the drape and pinned, be sure to mark the following key areas:
  - o Back bustline styleline
  - o Waistline at the Side Seam: Draw a crossmark
  - o Side Seam
  - o Hem: Follow the bottom of the Dress Form, making sure it is parallel to the floor.

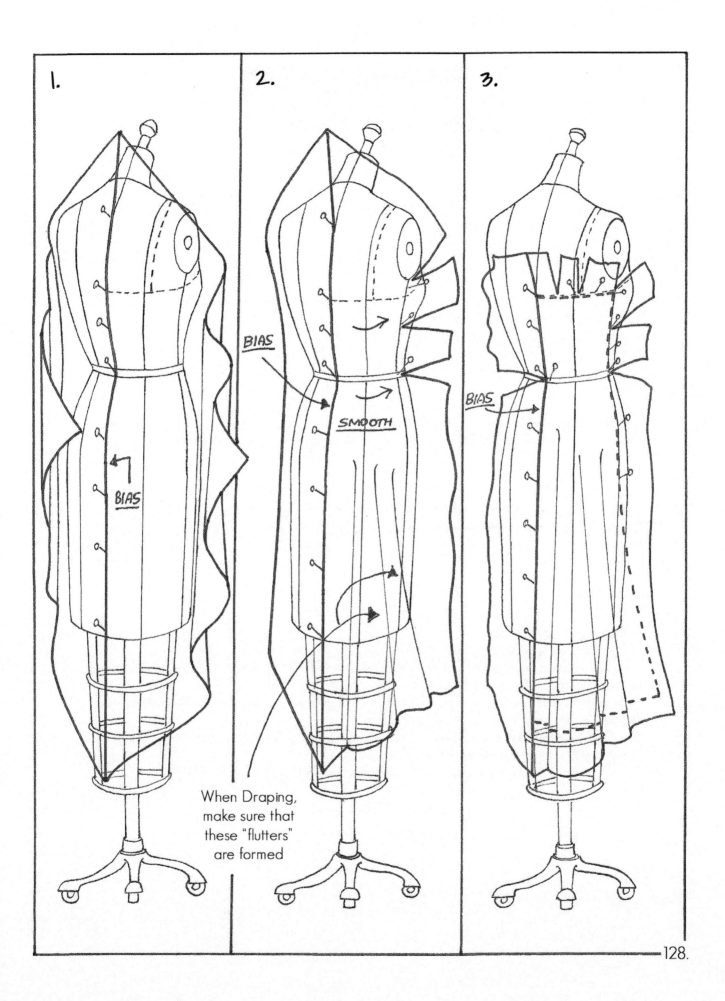

1.

2.

BIAS

BIAS

When Draping,
make sure that
these "flutters"
are formed

SMOOTH

3.

BIAS

Bias Slip Dress

TRUEING THE DRAPE

BALANCING THE TRACED DRAPE:

1. After draping the Bias Slip Dress, remove draped fabric from the Dress Form to place the BACK and FRONT draped fabric on Dotted Pattern Paper:
- Cut a piece of Dotted Pattern Paper 45" wide X 50" long.
- Before placing the fabric on the Dotted Paper:
  - -Draw a straight up-and-down CF Grainline 2" away from the right edge of the paper, and
  - -Draw a straight up-and-down CB Grainline 2" from the left edge of the paper.
- Carefully lie the draped fabric pieces by matching the CB Fold of the BACK dress to the CB Grainline, and then match the CF Fold of the FRONT dress to the CF Grainline.
- To hold the fabric pieces in place, you can either use tape, pins, or fabric weights.

2. Trace the Fabric drape onto the Dotted Pattern Paper:
- Using a Tracing Wheel, carefully trace the markings of your FRONT and BACK drapes onto the Dotted Pattern Paper.
- When tracing the markings, make sure you trace:
  - -Necklines/Top edges
  - -Side Seams
  - -Hem
  - -Crossmarks for the waist, hips
  - -If you draped a DART, then trace the dart location
- When finished tracing, remove the fabric from the Dotted Pattern Paper. If you used tape, carefully remove the tape so the paper does not ripp or become damaged.
- Double-check and make sure that you traced all the markings of your Bias Slip Dress drape as you remove the fabric from the Dotted Pattern Paper.
- Once you are secure in your tracings, it is recommended that you lightly go over your tracings with a pencil so you can see the marks better.
- Finally, cut the Dotted Pattern paper in half to separate the BACK from the FRONT.

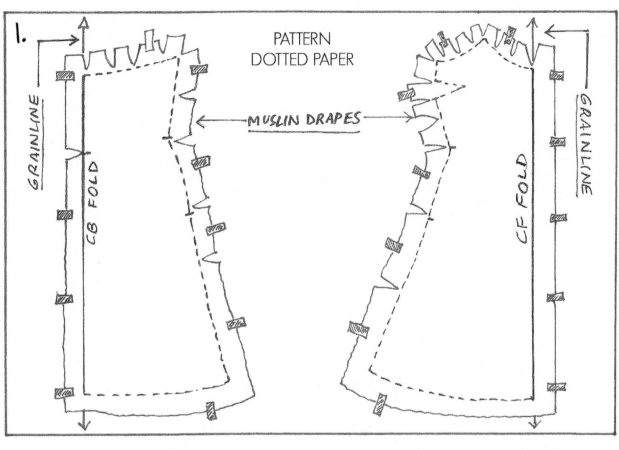

1.

PATTERN
DOTTED PAPER

GRAINLINE

CB FOLD

MUSLIN DRAPES

CF FOLD

GRAINLINE

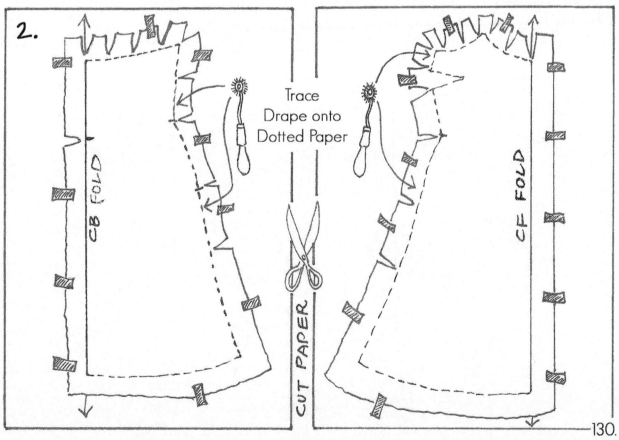

2.

CB FOLD

Trace
Drape onto
Dotted Paper

CUT PAPER

CF FOLD

3. If a Side Bust Dart was draped in your Bias Slip Dress drape, at this time, it is recommended to fold the dart closed. This will help in the TRUEING and BALANCING of your Bias Slip Dress drape.
- Carefully fold the dart as shown on image.
- Tape or pin to secure the folded dart.

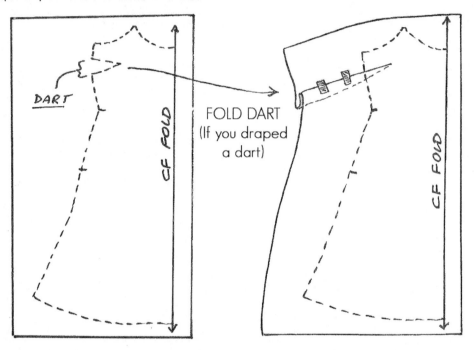

DART

CF FOLD

FOLD DART
(If you draped a dart)

CF FOLD

4. Next, lay BACK paper pattern ON TOP of the FRONT paper pattern:
- When placing the BACK paper on top of the FRONT paper, make sure to place paper patterns so the CENTER BACK of the traced dress pattern is PARALLEL to the CENTER FRONT of the traced dress pattern.
  - Match at the WAIST, as shown on image.

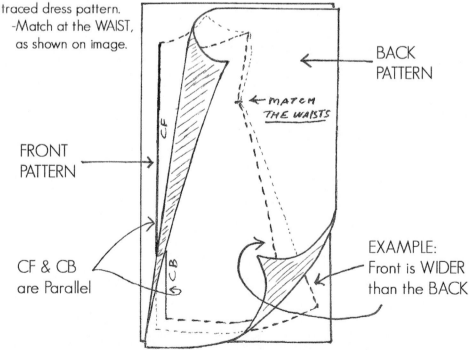

CF

CB

MATCH THE WAISTS

BACK PATTERN

FRONT PATTERN

CF & CB are Parallel

EXAMPLE: Front is WIDER than the BACK

5.

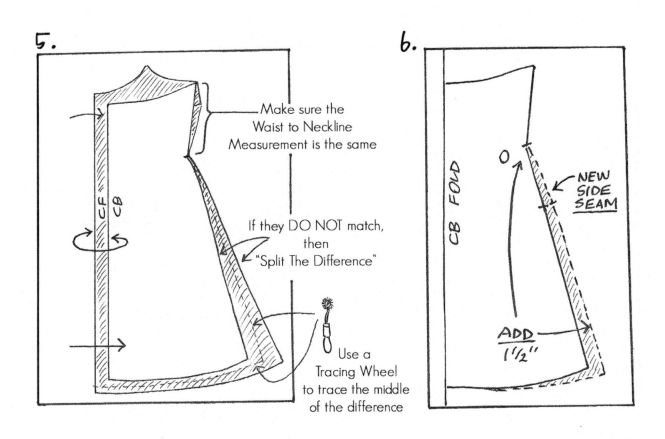

Make sure the Waist to Neckline Measurement is the same

If they DO NOT match, then "Split The Difference"

Use a Tracing Wheel to trace the middle of the difference

CF
CB

6.

CB FOLD

O

NEW SIDE SEAM

ADD 1½"

7.

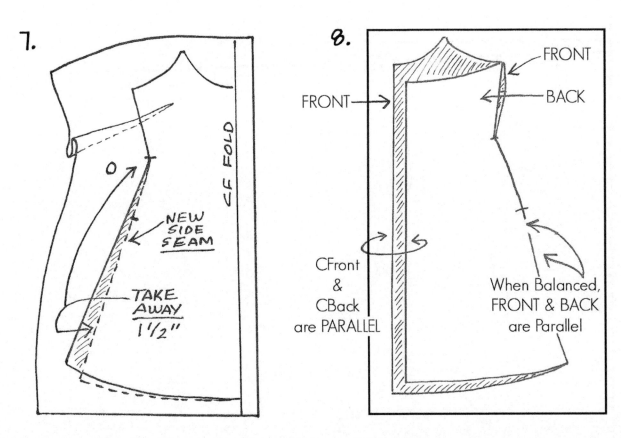

O

NEW SIDE SEAM

CF FOLD

TAKE AWAY 1½"

8.

FRONT

FRONT

BACK

CFront & CBack are PARALLEL

When Balanced, FRONT & BACK are Parallel

132.

1. True the Side Bust Dart (if you draped one) as shown below:

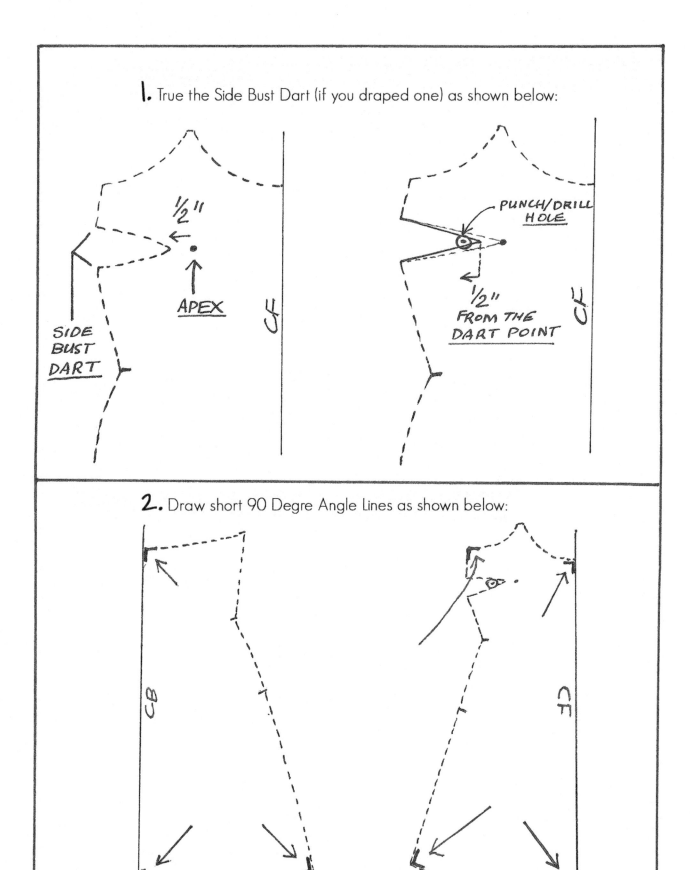

2. Draw short 90 Degre Angle Lines as shown below:

3. True the Waist:

DO:

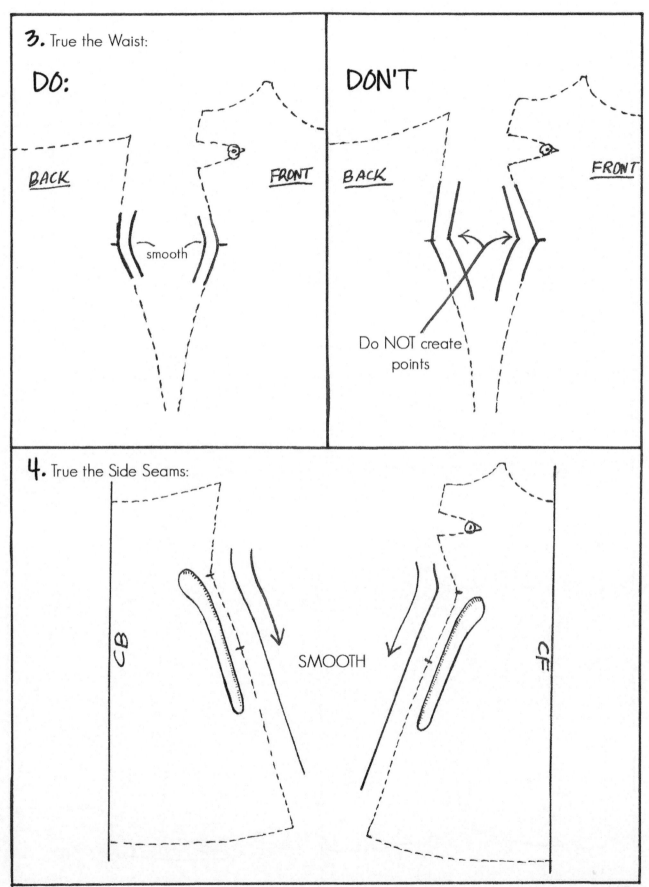

BACK   FRONT

smooth

DON'T

BACK   FRONT

Do NOT create points

4. True the Side Seams:

CB   SMOOTH   CF

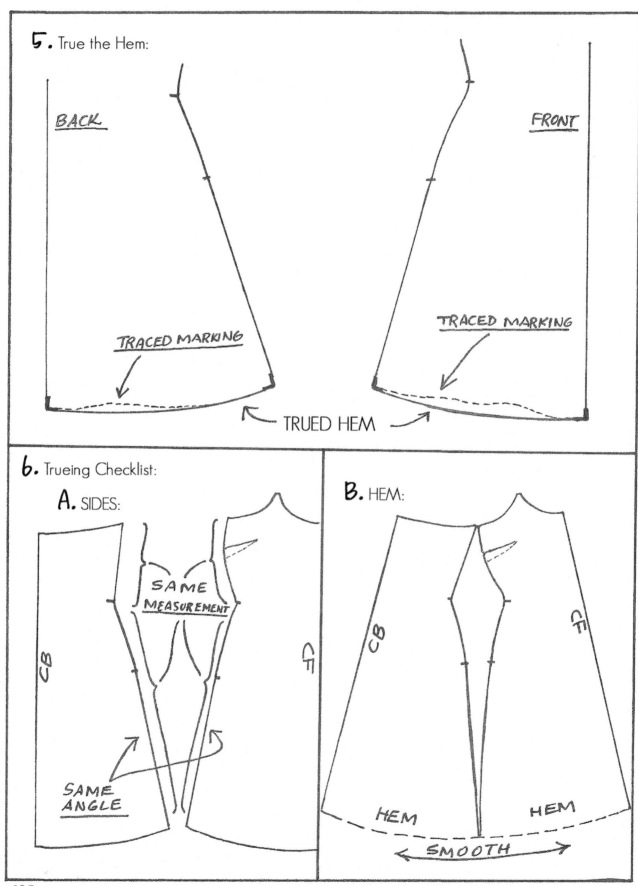

5. True the Hem:

BACK

FRONT

TRACED MARKING

TRACED MARKING

TRUED HEM

6. Trueing Checklist:

A. SIDES:

CB

CF

SAME MEASUREMENT

SAME ANGLE

B. HEM:

CB

CF

HEM

HEM

SMOOTH

135.

7. Add Seam Allowances and Notches

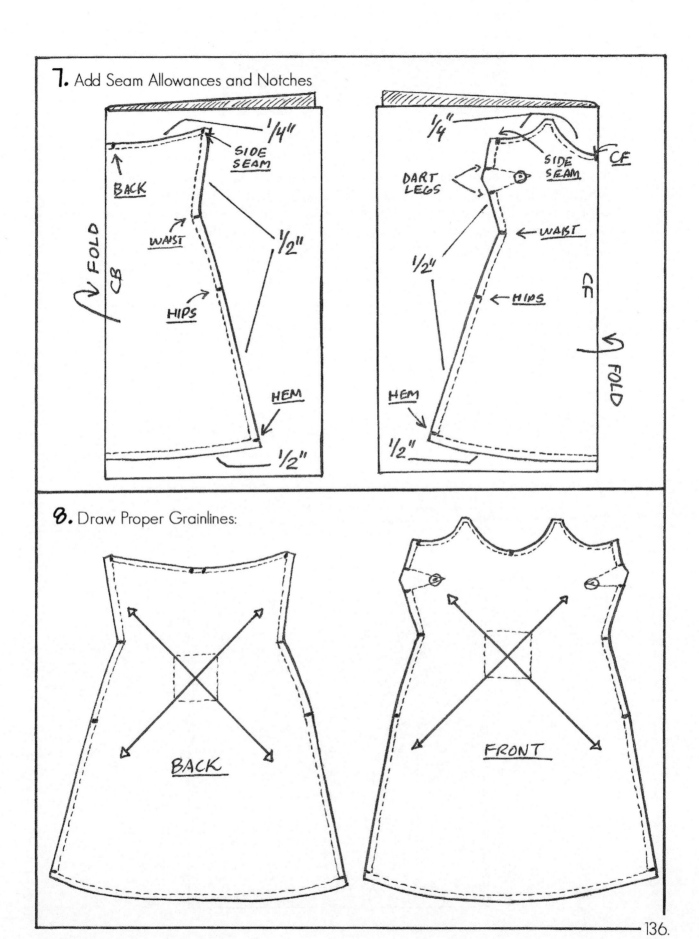

1/4"

SIDE SEAM

BACK

FOLD

CB

WAIST

1/2"

HIPS

HEM

1/2"

1/4"

DART LEGS

SIDE SEAM

CF

WAIST

1/2"

HIPS

CF

FOLD

HEM

1/2"

8. Draw Proper Grainlines:

BACK

FRONT

136.

Bias Slip Dress

CUTTING THE FABRIC

- After TRUEING your drape/pattern, add seam allowances to the Dotted Paper Pattern. Lay FULL front and FULL back pattern (as opposed to half), onto your fabric to cut.
- Use Dotted Paper (or brown craft paper) to aid in cutting. Lay the fabric and pattern on top of the paper--three layers total--and treat as one. Pin all 3 layers together.
- Pinning paper under the fabric will help in cutting and reduce the slipping of the fabric.

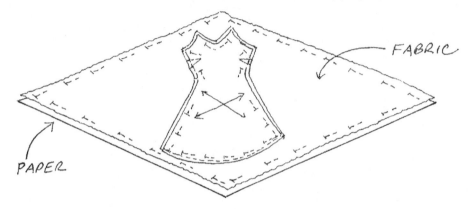

•Marker: Lay your Bias Patterns and Bias Strips with the grainline matching the selvage line.

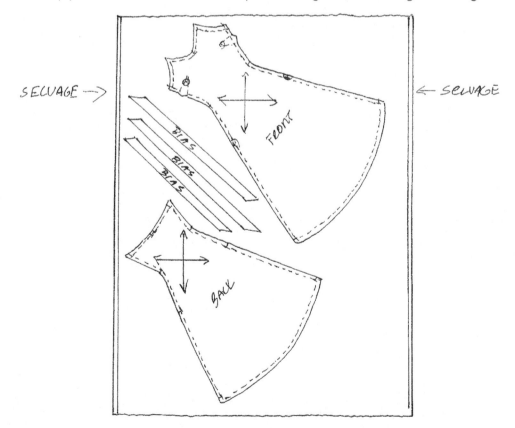

Bias Slip Dress

SEWING INSTRUCTIONS

1. Sew the Bust Darts. Make sure to sew 1/2" past the punch hole. Press dart down.

2. Sew FRONT to BACK at the side seams. First, pin carefully, making sure that the notches match, and the sew using 1/2" seam allowance. Press Open.

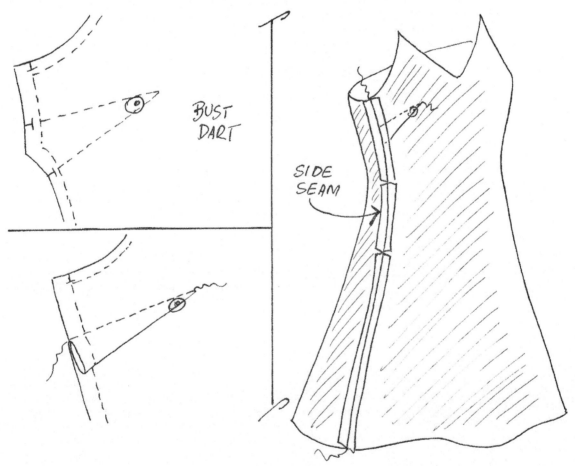

3. Sew your 1 1/4" Bias Strips together at 1/2" to create one long piece.

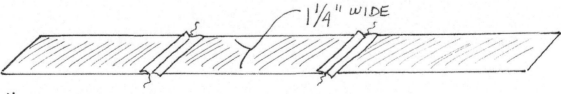

4. Fold Bias Strip over 1/4" at Top and Bottom.

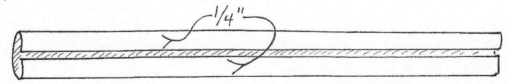

Bias Slip Dress

SEWING INSTRUCTIONS

5. Measure how long shoulder straps should be, and add 2" extra.

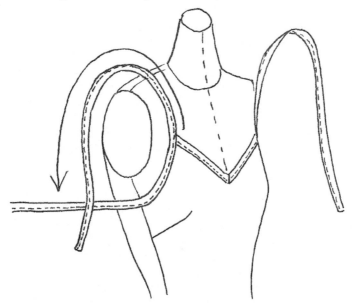

6. Fold Bias Binding over the raw edges of the top of the dress. To create a point in the CF, make sure to fold the bias binding like a dart.

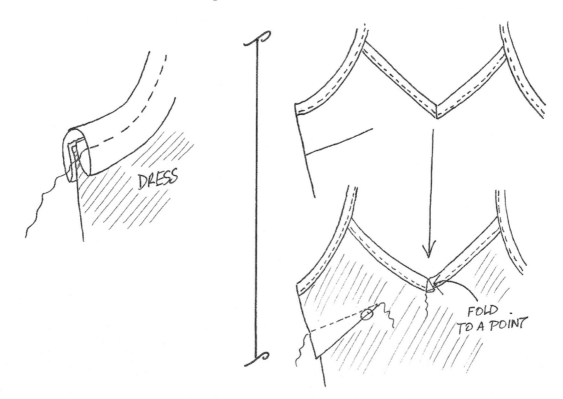

DRESS

FOLD TO A POINT

Bias Slip Dress
SEWING INSTRUCTIONS

7. Hang the Bias Slip Dress on a hanger or Dress Form before hemming to allow the bias to "grow".
- Because fabric will stretch on the bias, it is important to allow your garment to hang for a minimum of 24 hours prior to hemming.
- If, after 24 hours of hanging, the side seams have lengthened (sometimes they end up like pointed shapes), carefully pin or mark the entire hem to be parallel to the floor.
- Cut off any excess fabric to make the hem even.

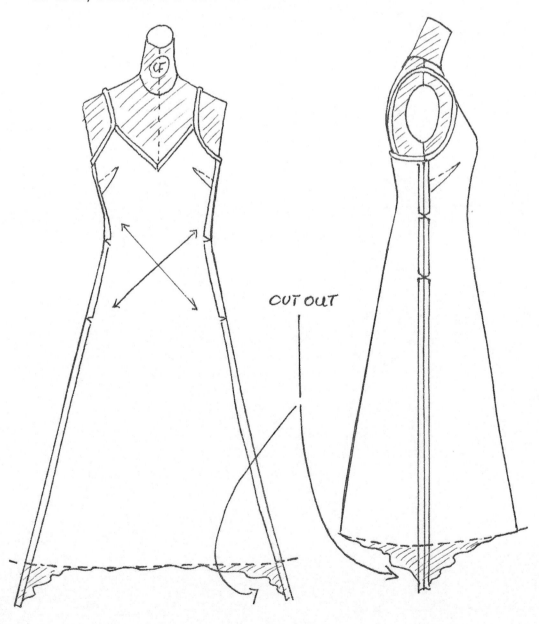

CUT OUT

Bias Slip Dress

SEWING INSTRUCTIONS

8. Hem your Bias Slip Dress. A baby hem or hem that is from 1/8" to 1/4" is the prefered method.

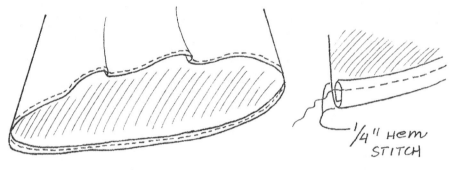

¹/₄" Hem STITCH

9. Finished Bias Slip Dress:

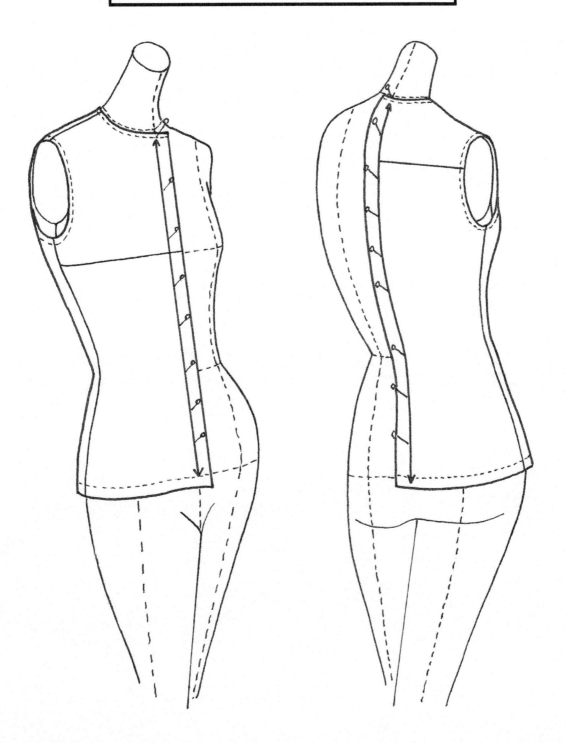

KNIT TOP

Knit Top

PREPARING THE FABRIC

- Prep the Knit Fabric for draping.
  - Cut 2 (two) knit pieces 30"L x 15W
  - Label one piece FRONT and one piece BACK

- Draw Straight Grainlines 1" away from the edges of each piece. These lines will represent the CB and CF accordingly.
  - BACK piece: Mark 3" down from the top edge. This is the neckline. Then mark 4" down from the 3" neckline mark. Draw a straight horizontal line, about 8" long. This line will represent the "Across Back" line and will keep the back drape balanced.
  - FRONT piece: Draw a straight horizontal line in the middle of the 30"L x 15"W piece of knit fabric. This will be placed across the bust area, parallel to the floor to keep the drape balanced.

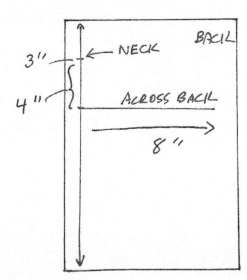

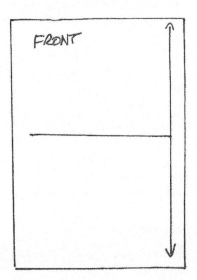

Knit Top

FRONT

1. After you have prepared the knit fabric for draping, take the FRONT cut fabric and pin the CF line of the fabric to the CF of the Dress Form.
- When you are pinning the fabric at the CF of the Dress Form, make sure the CROSSGRAIN line is at the BUST level. Pin down the CF, making sure the fabric is secure and not moving/shifting.
- A good pinning rule when securing the fabric at the CF or CB: Place pins 1" to 1 ½" apart so the fabric is secure.
- At the BUST level, smooth fabric over to APEX/Princess Line and place a pin there.
- Drape the FRONT NECKLINE, by using a process of pinning and clipping around the neckline. Clip into the fabric at neckline downwards until you hit the neckline of the Dress Form. The clipping will allow the fabric to properly smooth and drape around the NECK.

2. Drape the rest of the BUSTLINE, and then the SHOULDER, and FRONT ARMHOLE.
- Go back to the BUSTLINE and smooth the fabric across the rest of the BUSTLINE, making the sure the crossgrain line remains at the BUST level. Pin this line at the BUST level, up to the SIDE SEAM.
- NECKLINE: Once you have clipped and draped the NECKLINE, pin at the SHOULDER/NECK position.
- SHOULDER: Smooth the fabric up and over the SHOULDER seam of the Dress Form. Pin the fabric to the SHOULDER position of the Dress Form.
- ARMHOLE: Drape and smooth the fabric over the ARMHOLE ridge, past the ARMPLATE. Pin the fabric at the bottom of the ARMPLATE. Make sure when draping that you DO NOT PULL the fabric and that this area is smooth.
- If you find that there is extra ease when draping this area, carefully with your fingertips, drape the extra ease so it is smooth.

3. Drape the SIDE SEAM and MARK all the key areas.
- Keeping the crossgrain line at the BUST level, smooth all the excess fabric past the SIDE SEAM. Make sure to SMOOTH across the body of the Dress Form, and NOT PULL.
- Pin at the SIDE SEAM down to HIP level (about 7"-9" below the WAIST).
- To help with the draping and pinning, you can clip the fabric at certain points – at the WAIST for example, as shown.
- Pin at the HEM area as well.
- After you are satisfied with your drape, mark all the key areas of your FRONT drape:
  - Neckline
  - Shoulder (crossmark the shoulder tip)
  - Crossmark at Mid-Armhole
  - Crossmark 1" below Armplate
  - Side Seam
  - Crossmark at the Waist
  - Hem

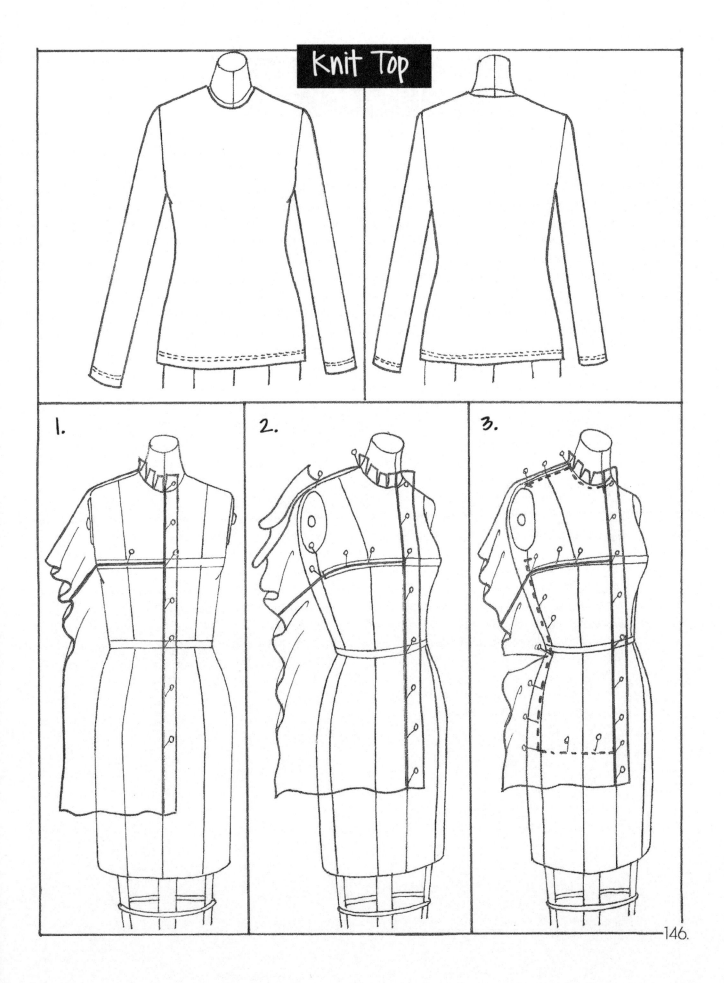

Knit Top

1.

2.

3.

146.

Knit Top

BACK

1. Take the BACK cut fabric and pin the CB line of the fabric to the CB of the Dress Form.
- When you are pinning the fabric at the CB of the Dress Form, make sure the CROSSGRAIN line is at the Shoulder Blade level. Pin down the CB, making sure the fabric is secure and not moving/shifting. Also, pin down the crossgrain line at the shoulder blade level.
- A good pinning rule when securing the fabric at the CF or CB: Place pins 1" to 1 ½" apart so the fabric is secure.
- Drape the BACK NECKLINE, by using a process of pinning and clipping around the neckline. Clip into the fabric at neckline downwards until you hit the neckline of the Dress Form. The clipping will allow the fabric to properly smooth and drape around the NECK.

2. Drape the BACK SHOULDER and SIDE SEAM.
- SHOULDER: After you have pinned the NECK area, drape and smooth the knit fabric up and over past the SHOULDER seam of the Dress Form. Pin at the SHOULDER seam.
- SIDE SEAM: Smooth all the excess knit fabric past the SIDE SEAM around the BACK upper torso area of the Dress Form, making sure NOT TO PULL, but carefully smoothing around the body, similar to what you did in the FRONT.

3. Pin the BACK drape and Mark all the key areas.
- After smoothing/draping the fabric around the back torso area past the SIDE SEAM, pin the fabric at the SIDE SEAM, from the bottom of the ARMPLATE, down to the HIP area (about 7"-9" below the WAIST).
- When smoothing and pinning, clip at the WAIST to help smooth the fabric past the SIDE SEAM and make the draping process easier; by clipping, it releases any fabric tension.
- Pin the HEM area of the fabric drape onto the Dress Form, around the HIP area.
- After you are satisfied with your drape, mark all the key areas of your BACK drape:
  - o Neckline
  - o Shoulder (crossmark the shoulder tip)
  - o Crossmark at Mid-Armhole
  - o Crossmark 1" below Armplate
  - o Side Seam
  - o Crossmark at the Waist
  - o Hem

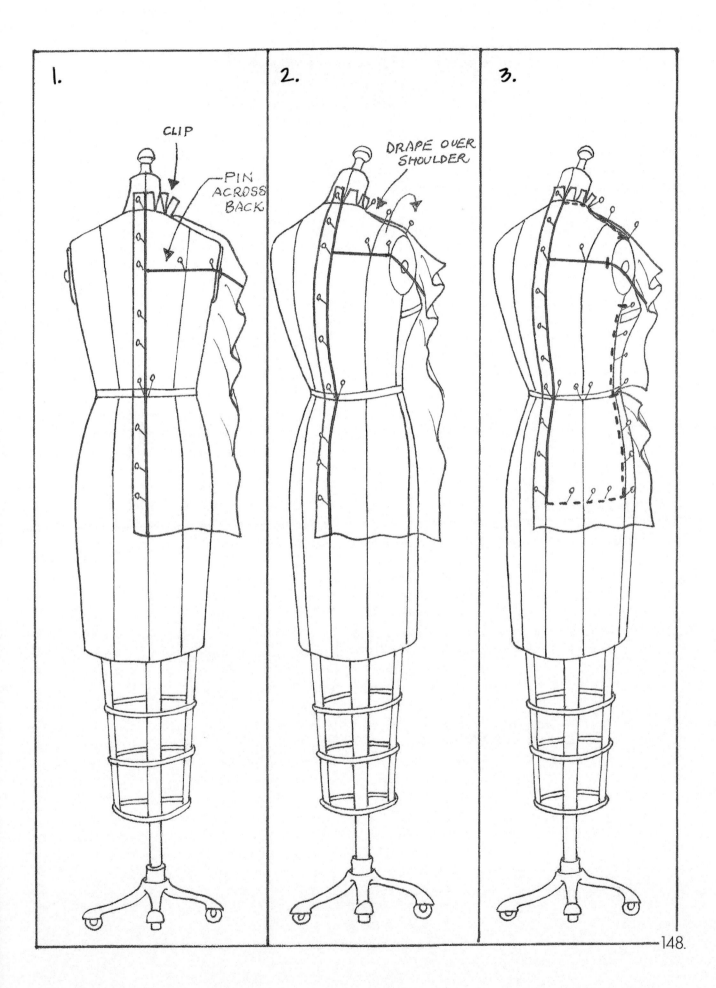

1.

CLIP

PIN
ACROSS
BACK

2.

DRAPE OVER
SHOULDER

3.

Knit Top

TRUEING AND BALANCING

- TRUEING-Front & Back:
  - -Transfer all markings that are on your Knit Drape onto Dotted Paper
  - -Lightly connect all your crossmarks and broken lines using a pencil so you can see a semblance of the pattern shape.

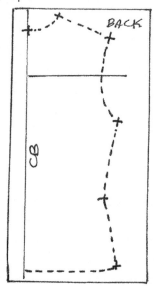 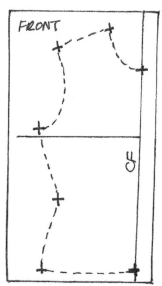

- BALANCING:
  - -Place Front Knit pattern on top of Back Knit pattern making sure the CF & CB are PARALLEL.
  - -Now check the sides and see if they are balanced and parallel as well.

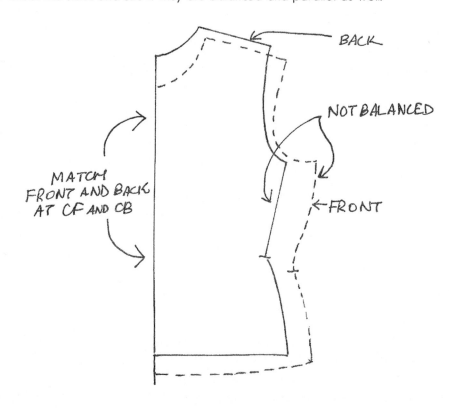

149.

BALANCING

• BALANCING (Continued):
  - Often, the FRONT drape is bigger or wider than the BACK drape or Visa Versa.
  - When this occurs, you need to TRUE the drape and make sure the FRONT & BACK are:
    o SAME Width
    o SAME Side Shape
    o SAME Shoulder Width Length

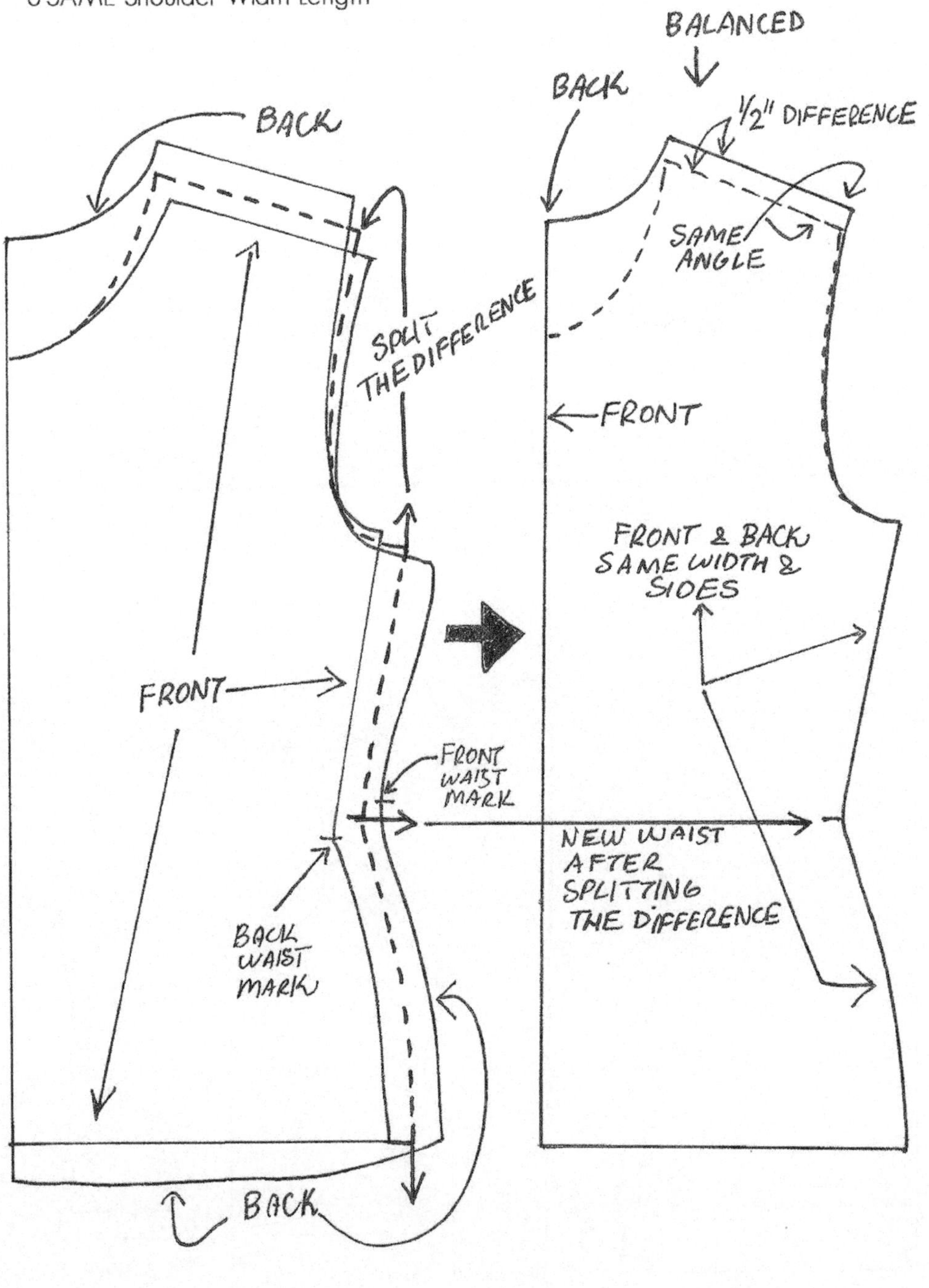

BACK

BALANCED

BACK

½" DIFFERENCE

SAME ANGLE

SPLIT THE DIFFERENCE

←FRONT

FRONT & BACK SAME WIDTH & SIDES

FRONT→

FRONT WAIST MARK

NEW WAIST AFTER SPLITTING THE DIFFERENCE

BACK WAIST MARK

BACK

Knit Top

SEAM ALLOWANCES & NOTCHES

- SEAM ALLOWANCES:
    - Once the Draped Pattern Pieces are TRUED, you can add seam allowances.
    - Knit garments get 1/4" seam allowances for all seams EXCEPT the Hem, which gets 1" seam allowance.

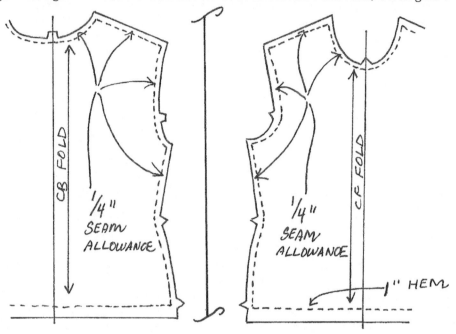

- NOTCHES:
    - Notches for Knit garment are POINTED or SQUARED
        o For BACK Neckline and Armhole use SQUARED NOTCH
        o For FRONT Neckline and Armole use POINTED NOTCH
        o For the WAIST and HEM use POINTED NOTCHES

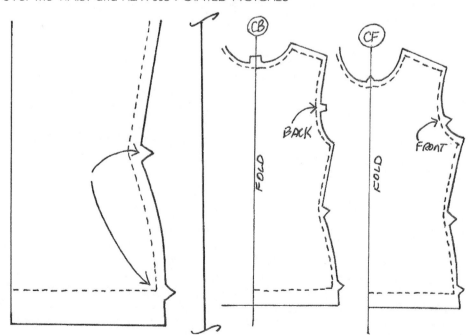

Knit Top

SEWING INSTRUCTIONS

- For sewing knits, use the Overlock Machine. The overlock machine sews and finishes the raw edge of the seam allowance all at once and is suitable for KNIT fabrics because it allows for stretch.

- If you do not have access to an Overlock Machine, you can use a Zig-Zag stitch on a home sewing machine.

- If you use a regular stitch on a home or industrial sewing machine, understand that when the fabric stretches, the stitch may snap/break and while sewing, your stitch will potentially skip.

1. Sew the FRONT to the BACK at the side seams:
   - Your seam allowances will be 1/4" which is what you will need when using the Overlock Machine. Press side seams lightly.

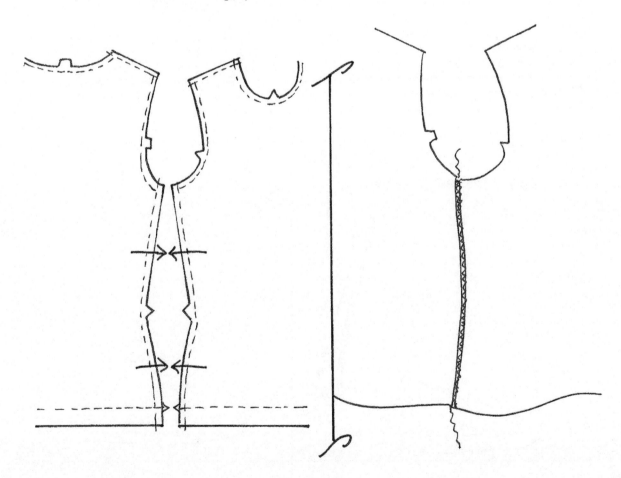

Knit Top

SEWING INSTRUCTIONS

2. Sew the Shoulder Seams:
  - Again, your seam allowances will be 1/4". Just place the seams (right sides together) and sew together using the overlock machine. Press lightly.

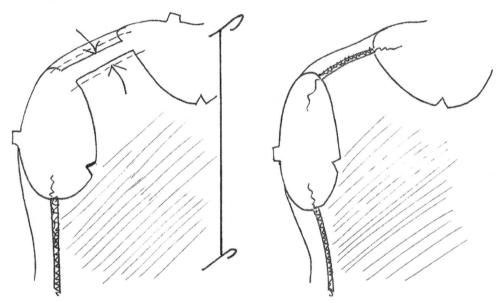

3. Sew the Hem of the top:
  - Use the Coverstitch machine to hem your top. The width of the hem is 1".
  - If you do not have access to a coverstitch machine you can use a Zig-Zag stitch to finish the hem. You can also use a twin-needle that can be purchased and attach to your home sewing machine. This provides a similar result to the coverstitch.
  - After sewing, lightly press the hem.

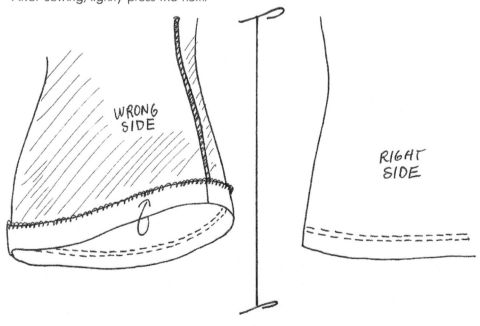

WRONG SIDE

RIGHT SIDE

Knit Top

SEWING INSTRUCTIONS

4. Sew the Sleeves:
- First, sew the underarm sleeve at 1/4" using the overlock machine.
- Then, match the notches of the sleeve cap to the notches on the armhole of the top and sew together at 1/4" using the overlock machine. Press lightly.

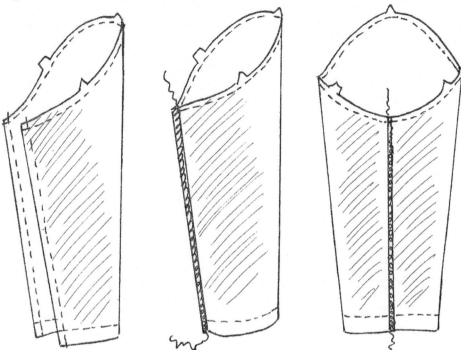

5. Sew the Hem of the Sleeves:
- Just like the hem of the top, the width of the hem is 1". Follow the same steps as the the hem of the top and use the Coverstitch Machine, Zig-Zag stitch or Twin Needle.

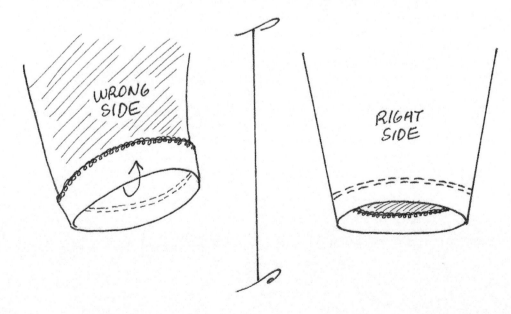

WRONG SIDE

RIGHT SIDE

Knit Top

SEWING INSTRUCTIONS

6. Ribbed Neckband:
- Create a Pattern piece for the Rib Knit Fabric. This will be shaped similar to a rectangle.
  - For measurements, first measure the entire neckline of the top. If it measures around 16", make the length of the rib neckband pattern 14"
- The length of the rib neckline pattern is usually 2" to 3" SHORTER than the actual neckline. This is because the rib knit stretches more than the regular knit and it allows for the neckband to lay smoother and better on the neckline.

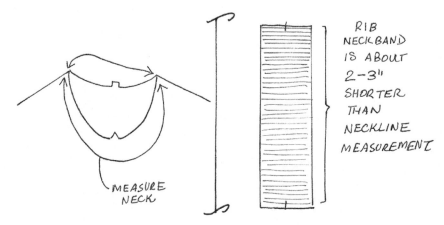

7. Finished Ribbed Neckband:
- Attach neckband to the knit top using an Overlock Stitch. Press lightly.

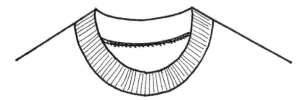

8. Finished Knit Top (with and without ribbed neckband):

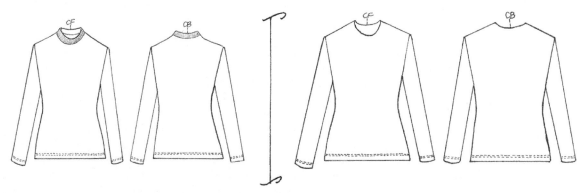

Sculpted Wrap Dress

Sculpted Wrap Dress

PREPARING THE FABRIC

1. Cut THREE (3) muslin pieces;
    -50" L x 45" W--Label "LEFT FRONT"
    -50" L x 45" W--Label "RIGHT FRONT"
    -50" L x 15" W--Label "BACK" (will drape HALF of BACK)

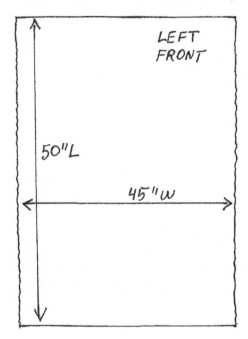

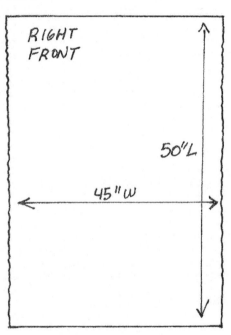

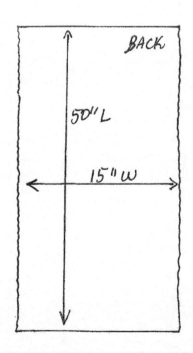

Sculpted Wrap Dress

PREPARING THE FABRIC

2. You will drape each side of the front separately beginning with the LEFT side of the Dress form (your right side when facing the form). This dress design has an asymmetrical front, therefore each side of the front will be draped separately.

    -Prep the 50" L x 45" W muslin piece labeled LEFT FRONT by drawing a vertical straight grainline down the CENTER of the muslin piece. Set aside.

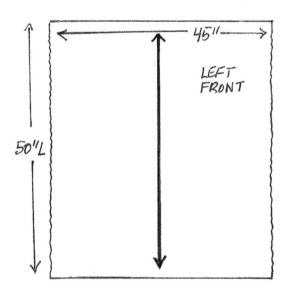

3. For the RIGHT FRONT 50" L x 45" W muslin piece, measure 10" from the LEFT EDGE and draw a vertical straight line from the TOP to the BOTTOM of the musline piece. Set aside.

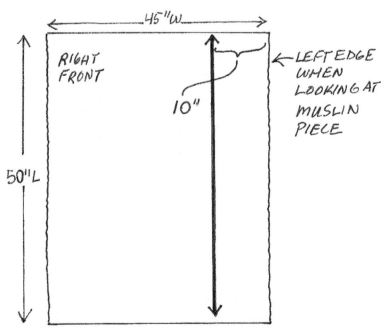

Sculpted Wrap Dress

PREPARING THE FABRIC

4. To prep the BACK 50"L x 15" W muslin piece:
   -Draw a vertical straight grainline 1" away from the left edge of the muslin.
   -From the top edge of muslin piece, measure 3" down and mark. Label NECKLINE.
   -Measure 4" down from 3" NECKLINE mark, and mark. Label ACROSS BACK.
   -lastly, go to the iron and press/fold the 1" CB grainline in. This will be your CENTER BACK.
   -Set aside.

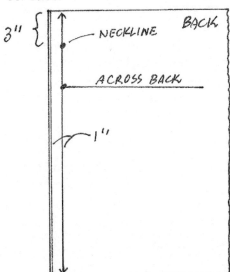
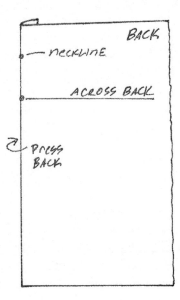

5. Mark the NECKLINE shape as well as the ARMHOLE shape of the draped dress design using Drape/Marking Tape. Pin tape to the dress form. If you do not have Drape/Marking Tape, cut 1/4" wide strips of muslin, about 45" long. You will use this tape as a helpful guide for your drape.

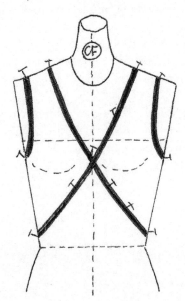

Sculpted Wrap Dress

FRONT DRAPE

6. Begin by draping the LEFT FRONT SIDE
   - This section of the FRONT of the Dress, will be the "Under" Front Dress that will go from the LEFT side of the body to the right and does NOT have any pleats.
   - There will be another draped section that will eventually go ON TOP of this section.

A) Place the DRAPING/MARKING TAPE onto the Dress Form to show the style line markings.
   - If you do not have draping/marking tape, you can use straight pins and pin the Dress Form along the desired style lines.
   - Mark the style lines along the NECKLINE and ARMHOLE as shown.
   - Make sure the draping tape ends 1" below the Armplate.

B) Place the 50" Long X 45" Wide cut piece of muslin labeled "LEFT FRONT" so that the straight grainline in the middle lines up with the CENTER FRONT/CF of the Dress Form.
   - Make sure the top edge of the cut muslin is level with the top of the Dress Form (above the neck area).
   - Pin the CF grainline on the CF of the Dress Form, starting from the CF NECK, down to the bottom of the Dress Form.
   - To make sure the cut muslin is secure to the Dress Form, make sure to pin on the Dress Form every 1 ½"-2" along the CF.

C) Begin draping the LEFT HALF of the FRONT of the Dress Form (RIGHT side if you are looking at the Dress Form).
   - Begin clipping the FRONT NECKLINE at the CF Bust level (you can remove any pins above this point).
   - Clip every 2" following the style line marking on the Dress Form. As you clip, make sure to secure a pin where you have clipped, on the style line. Smooth and drape the fabric at the midriff/stomach area, continuing to clip and pin to the WAIST/SIDE SEAM position. Discard any excess muslin after clipping.
   - Next, smooth and drape the fabric across the RIGHT FRONT half of the Dress Form, from the WAIST, down to the bottom of the Dress Form. Make sure the fabric and CF grainline does not shift/move and is secure. If the fabric becomes loose, re-pin the CF to secure it.
   - As you smooth across the Dress Form, pin the fabric at the SIDE SEAM and clip it as well to release any draping tension.

6. Begin by draping the LEFT FRONT SIDE

A.

Style Line
Markings

1"
Below
Armplate

B.

Grainline   Pin CF

C.

Drape
This Side
First

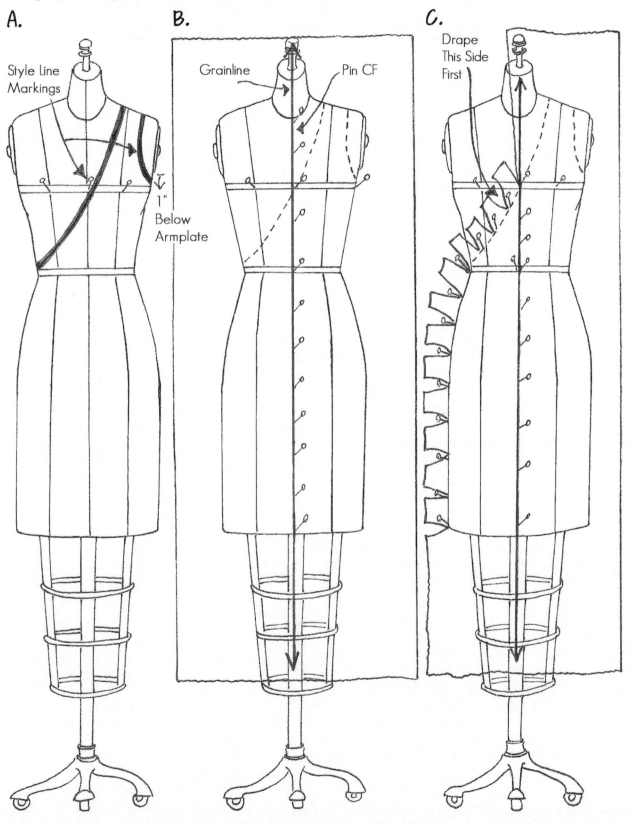

Sculpted Wrap Dress

FRONT DRAPE

6.-continued

D) Go back to the CF Bust Level and now it is time to drape the other section of this half of the Dress.

- Starting at the CF/Bust level, smooth the fabric above the bust to the SHOULDER and ARMHOLE. As you drape and smooth, continue the "Clip & Pin" method you did for steps B) and C). Clip and pin the following:
  - Neckline
  - Shoulder
  - Armhole
- Discard any excess fabric after clipping.

E) Smooth and drape the other side of this section of the Dress.

- Making sure the CF grainline and pins are secured, smooth the fabric past the SIDE seam over the BUST.
- SIDE BUST DART: As you smooth, it will become evident that you will need to drape a side bust DART in order for the fabric to lay smoothly over the bust of the Dress Form. Fold a small dart beginning about 1 ½"-2" below the Armhole style line at the SIDE SEAM (See "Close-up" Image). Fold the dart until the area is smooth. Pin it down at the SIDE SEAM.
- Continue smoothing the fabric from the center front (CF) towards the side seam. Smooth the fabric from the bust dart towards the waist, and then continue downwards until you reach the bottom of the form.
- As you smooth past the SIDE SEAM, clip and pin every 2" to release draping tension and allow for smoother draping.
- Once you drape toward the bottom of the Dress Form, you can mark the shape of the hem; here it is an asymmetrical hem. You can lightly mark this with a pencil and/or marker.
- Discard any excess muslin, after you have clipped, pinned, and draped.

F) Mark the Style Lines:

- Mark the following:
  - Front Neckline
  - Shoulder
  - Armhole
  - Left Side Seam
  - Right Side Seam
  - Dart: Crossmark where the Dart folds are, at the Side Seam
  - Lightly mark the actual dart as folded
  - Mark DART POINT, about 1" away from Bust Apex
  - Waist: Crossmark the waist on both sides
  - Hem: Re-mark the desired hem shape

*Before you drape the other FRONT section of the Sculpted Wrap Dress, you can carefully remove this drape from the Dress Form.

163.

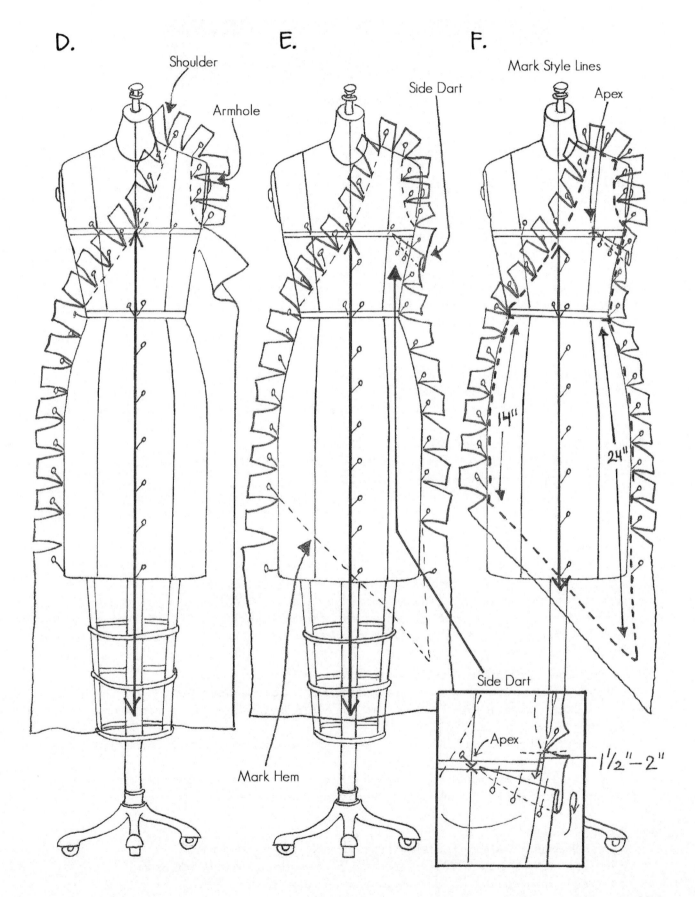

D.

Shoulder

Armhole

E.

Side Dart

Mark Hem

F.

Mark Style Lines

Apex

14"

24"

Side Dart

Apex

1½"–2"

Sculpted Wrap Dress

FRONT DRAPE

7. Drape the "RIGHT" FRONT of the Dress.
- Eventually this drape will go ON TOP of the last draped section of the FRONT of the Dress.

A) Place the DRAPING/MARKING TAPE onto the Dress Form to show the style line markings
as shown in image:
- If you do not have draping/marking tape, you can use straight pins and pin the
Dress Form along the desired style lines.
- Mark the style lines along the NECKLINE and ARMHOLE as shown.

B) Position the muslin piece labeled as "RIGHT FRONT," which measures 50" in length and 45" in width,
in such a way that the straight grainline, located 10" away from the left edge of the fabric, aligns with
the CENTER FRONT/CF of the Dress Form.
- Make sure the top edge of the cut muslin is level with the top of the Dress Form
(above the neck area).
C) Place a pin (or 2) at the BUST level, shown, while holding the cut piece of muslin, making
sure the up-and-down grainline remains at CF.
- Clip from the top edge, down to the CF BUST level, where the pins are. This will allow for easier draping.

D) Begin draping this section of the FRONT Sculpted Wrap Dress.
- Begin by clipping and pinning the NECKLINE area, from the CF BUST to the SHOULDER.
- Next, clip and pin the SHOULDER.
- Next, clip and pin the ARMHOLE area, making sure the upper bust section is smooth.
- Next, go back to the FRONT area at the MIDRIFF, and carefully clip and pin so that the midriff section is
smooth. Pin at the WAIST/SIDE SEAM.
- Go back to the other SIDE SEAM, and begin pinning under the ARMPLATE, smoothing and draping down
the SIDE SEAM. While you are doing this, you can begin draping the SIDE PLEATS on the other side.
- In conjunction with draping the SIDE PLEATS on one side of the Dress Form, you are also smoothing the
other side (the non-pleated side), placing pins at the SIDE SEAM, WAIST, clipping as you smooth. The
draping process is one of: Draping the side pleats, pinning, and then smoothing the other side, and pinning.
- As you drape, you will notice the muslin fabric shifting, so that the up-and-down grainline will eventually
shift toward one side of the Dress Form.
E) Continue draping the SIDE PLEATS until you are satisfied with the design/style.
- Normally, this design has six (6) pleats but depending on the design/drape, there could be more or less.
- As you drape and pin the SIDE PLEATS on one SIDE SEAM, always make sure the non-pleated SIDE SEAM
is smooth, as you proceed to pin it.
- IMPORTANT: When draping DO NOT PULL the fabric; instead, smooth the fabric on the Dress Form.

F) Once you are finished draping, cut excess muslin fabric and mark the desired hem shape; here it is an
asymmetrical shape, just like the one you draped on the first drape (the "LEFT" Front).

G) Mark the Style Lines:
- Front Neckline • Shoulder • Armhole Right Side Seam (non-pleated side)
- Left Side Seam (pleated side) • Crossmark the Waist on the non-pleated Side Seam
- Crossmark the pleat folds (so when you take the drape out you know where the pleats are)
- Hem: Re-mark the desired hem shape

7. Drape the "RIGHT" FRONT of the Dress.

Mark Style Lines

A.

B.

10"

Pin
Grainline
at CF Bustline

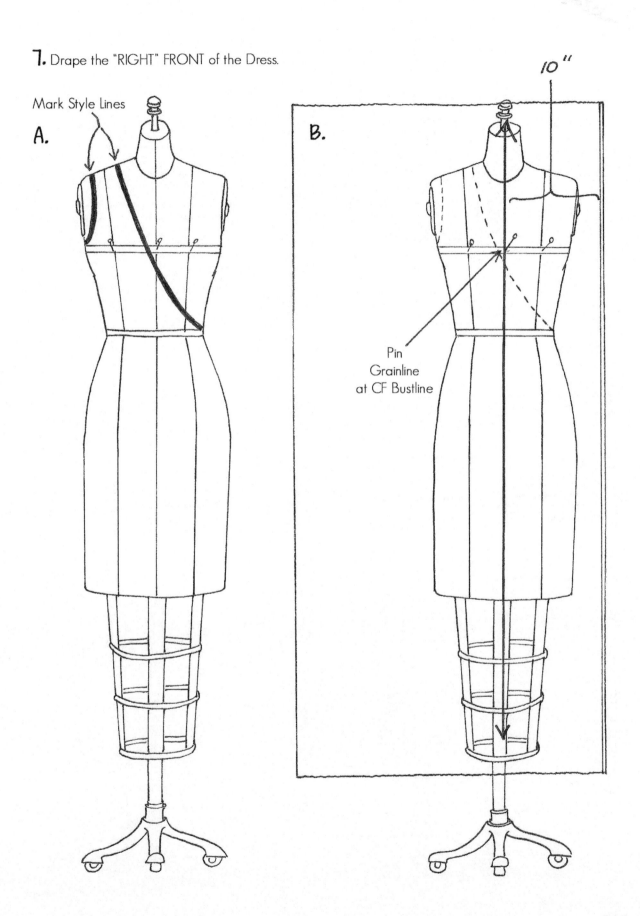

C.   D.

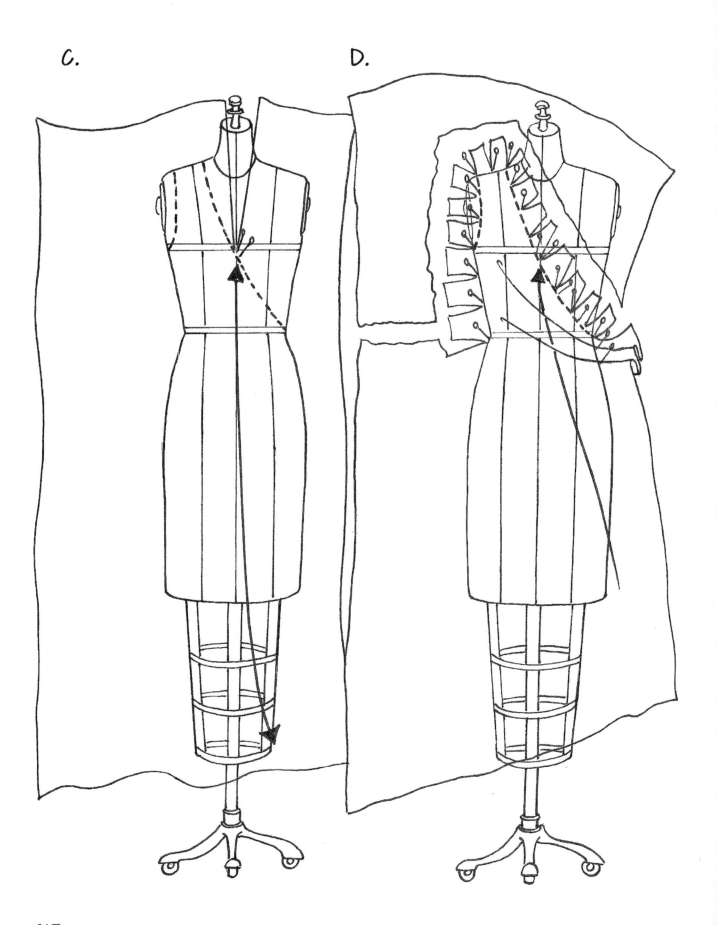

167.

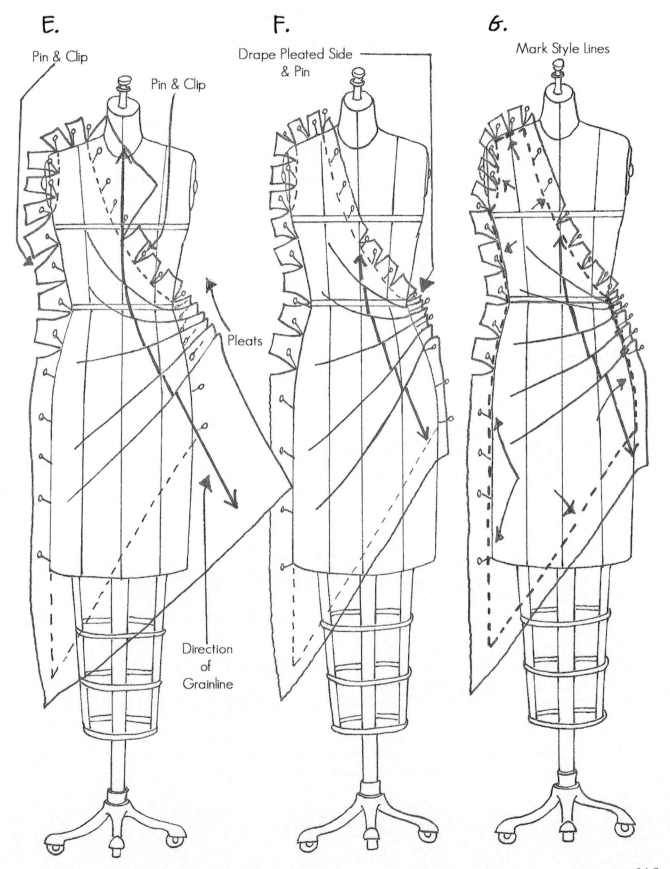

E.

Pin & Clip

Pin & Clip

Pleats

Direction
of
Grainline

F.

Drape Pleated Side
& Pin

G.

Mark Style Lines

168.

Sculpted Wrap Dress

BACK DRAPE

8.

Drape the BACK:
- For the back drape, you will only need to drape HALF of the Dress since the RIGHT side is the same as the LEFT.
- Traditionally when draping only one half of the BACK, the RIGHT side of the BACK of the Dress Form (as you are looking at it) is the side that is draped.

A) Using the Draping Tape, mark the NECKLINE and ARMHOLE of the Back Dress. If you do not have Draping Tape, you can just use straight pins, or cut strips of Muslin and pin those to mark the NECKLINE and ARMHOLE.

B) Begin draping the BACK.
- Place "BACK PIECE" of 50" L X 15" W cut muslin on the BACK Dress Form.
- Align the cut muslin piece so:
  - The CB grainline (that is folded 1" away from edge) is at the CB of the Dress Form.
  - Match the NECKLINE crossmark on the cut muslin with CB NECKLINE of the Dress Form.
- Pin down the CB of the Dress Form, placing a pin every 1 ½"-2". Pin down to the bottom of the Dress Form.
- Next, pin the "Across Back" crossgrain line across the top back/shoulder blade area of the Dress Form. As you are pinning, make sure this line stays PARALLEL to the floor. Pin to the ARMHOLE, as shown.

C) Continue, and finish the BACK drape.
- Clip and smooth the NECK area to the NECKLINE mark. Pin the NECKLINE up to the SHOULDER. Remove any excess muslin fabric.
- Drape muslin fabric over the SHOULDER and pin. Cut excess muslin fabric.
- Smooth fabric to the ARMHOLE, across the top back area. Clip and pin around the ARMHOLE area.
- Next, drape/smooth the muslin fabric below the ARMHOLE from the CB to the SIDE SEAM. Clip and pin at the SIDE SEAM, to the WAIST. Remove any excess muslin fabric.
- When draping the WAIST area, DO NOT PULL TIGHTLY but SMOOTH it to the SIDE SEAM. If you want, you can drape a fisheye DART at the WAIST/Princess Seam area for a more fitted shape. But if the fabric is jersey knit or silky/satin, a DART may not be necessary.
- Continue draping the rest of the BACK, from the WAIST to the bottom of the Dress Form, smoothing NOT PULLING to the SIDE SEAM. Clip and pin down the SIDE SEAM.

8. Drape Back: Half of Back

A.

B.

BACK

C.

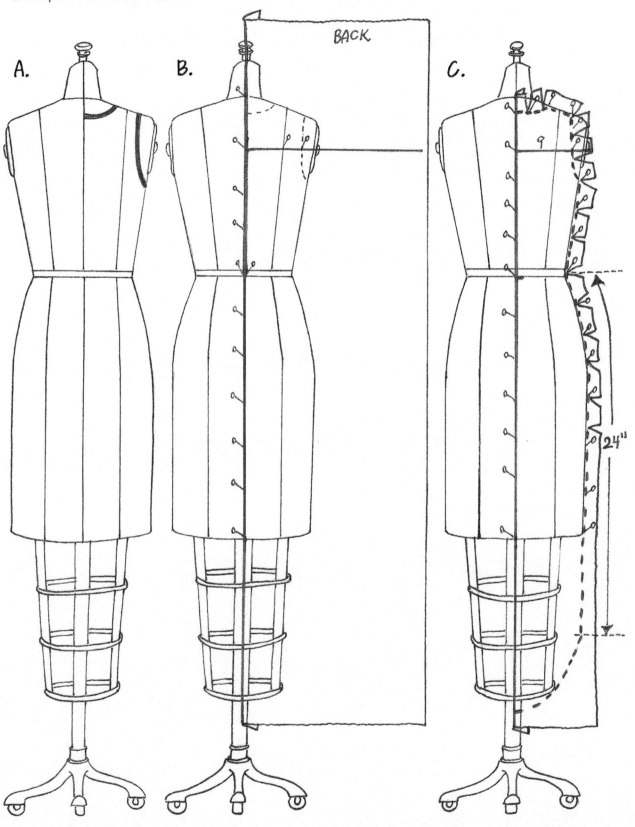

24"

Sculpted Wrap Dress
TRUEING THE DRAPE

9. How to TRUE the pleats in the Dress Drape:
   A. Transfer muslin draped piece onto Dotted Paper, use the Tracing Wheel to transfer marks.
   B. Transfer PLEAT marks on Dotted Paper.

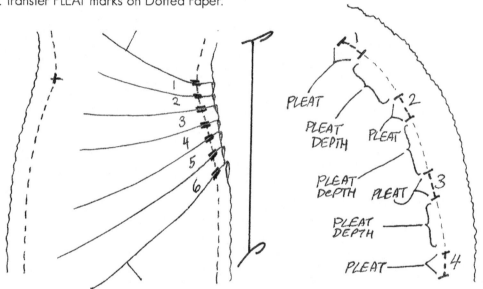

C. On Dotted Paper, FOLD pleats as shown and use Tracing Wheel to trace the folded pleats:

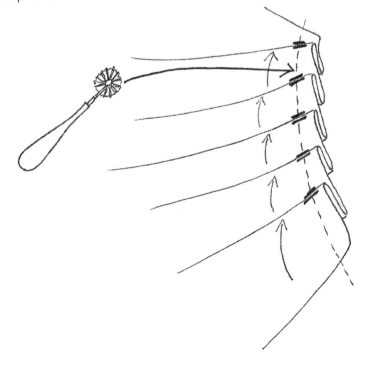

Sculpted Wrap Dress

TRUEING THE DRAPE

D. Open folded PLEATS on the Dotted Paper to get the proper shapes:

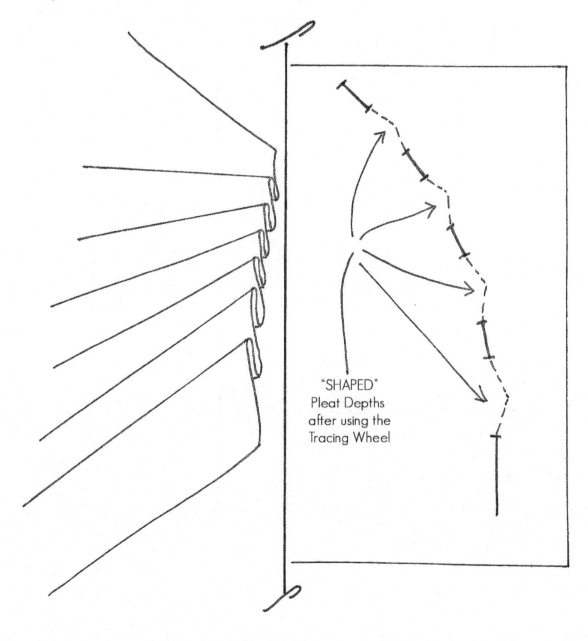

"SHAPED"
Pleat Depths
after using the
Tracing Wheel

Sculpted Wrap Dress

TRUEING THE DRAPE

10. Finish TRUEING of the dress and add seam allowance and hem to your patterns.:

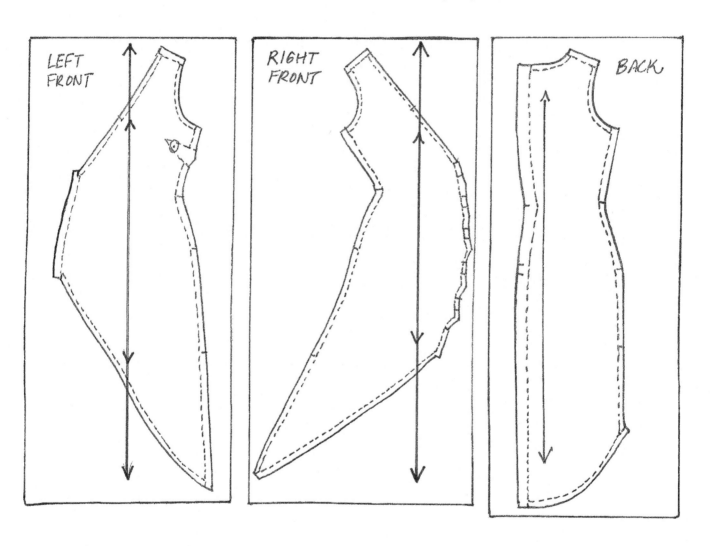

LEFT FRONT

RIGHT FRONT

BACK

Sculpted Wrap Dress

NECKLINE FACINGS

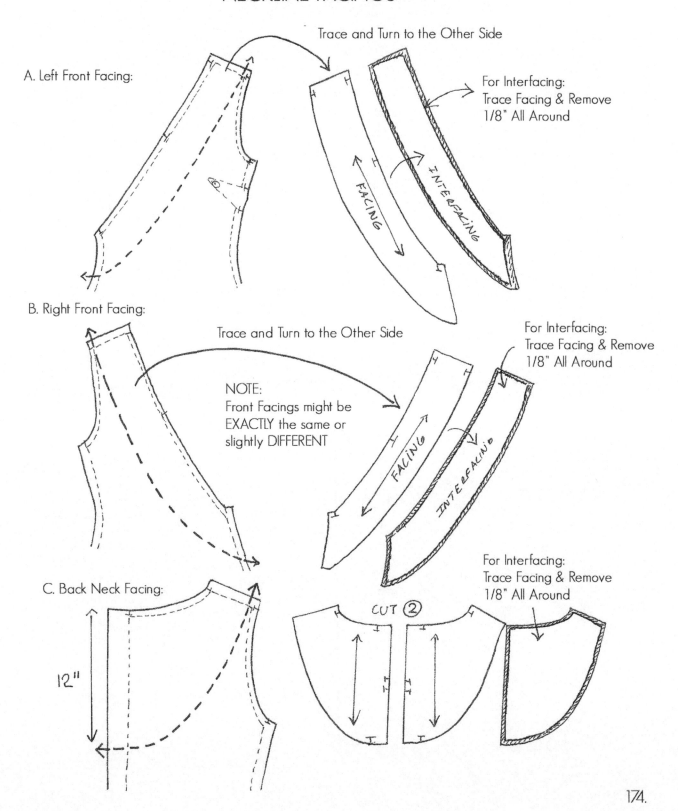

Trace and Turn to the Other Side

A. Left Front Facing:

For Interfacing:
Trace Facing & Remove
1/8" All Around

FACING

INTERFACING

B. Right Front Facing:

Trace and Turn to the Other Side

NOTE:
Front Facings might be
EXACTLY the same or
slightly DIFFERENT

For Interfacing:
Trace Facing & Remove
1/8" All Around

FACING

INTERFACING

For Interfacing:
Trace Facing & Remove
1/8" All Around

C. Back Neck Facing:

12"

CUT ②

Sculpted Wrap Dress

SEWING INSTRUCTIONS

1. Sew DARTS (if any) as marked on the LEFT FRONT. Press the fold of the dart downwards:

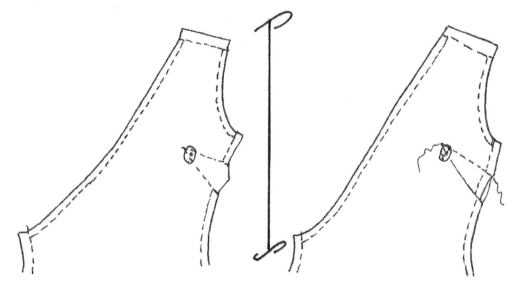

2. Sew PLEATS down on the RIGHT FRONT, using a 3/8" staystitch:

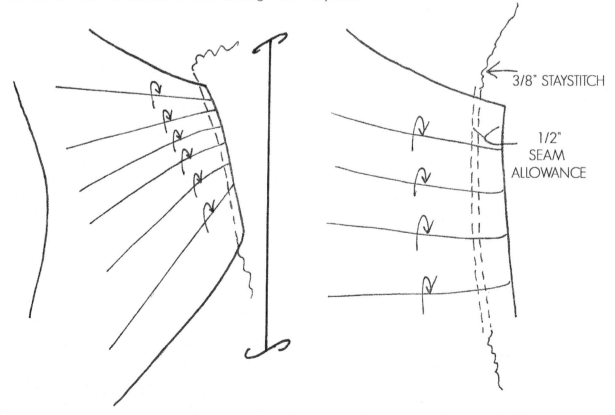

3/8" STAYSTITCH

1/2"
SEAM
ALLOWANCE

Sculpted Wrap Dress

SEWING INSTRUCTIONS

3. Sew SHOULDERS, front pieces to back pieces, using 1/2" seam allowance. Press seam open:

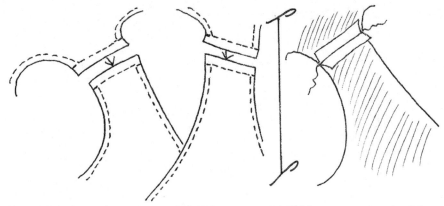

4. Sew FACINGS: Begin by sewing FRONT facings to BACK facings at the shoulders using 1/2" seam allowance. Press shoulder seams open.

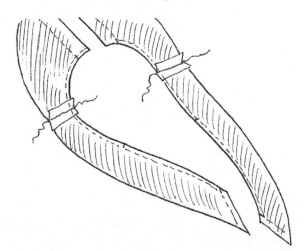

5. Sew the facings to the FRONT and BACK neckline of the dress using 1/4" seam allowance. Understitch and Press.

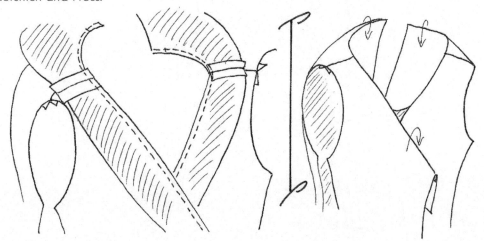

Sculpted Wrap Dress

SEWING INSTRUCTIONS

6. Staystitch Front Dress pieces. Both on the RIGHT and LEFT sides of the dress using a 3/8" stitch:

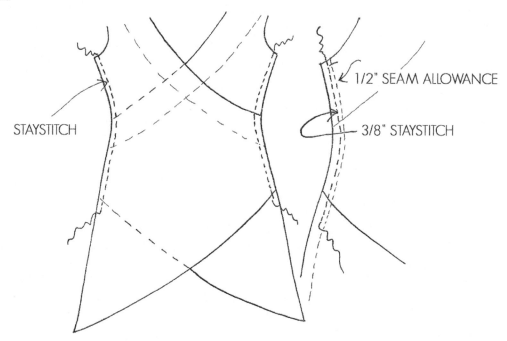

STAYSTITCH

1/2" SEAM ALLOWANCE

3/8" STAYSTITCH

7. Sew the FRONT Dress to the BACK Dress at the SIDE SEAMS using a 1/2" seam allowance. Press seams open:

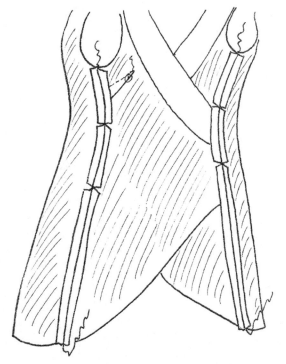

Sculpted Wrap Dress
SEWING INSTRUCTIONS

8. Sew CENTER BACK seam using a 1" seam allowance. Sew from the hem to the double notches around the hip area (where the zipper opening will end). Leave the rest of the CB open to sew the zipper. Press CB seam allowance open:

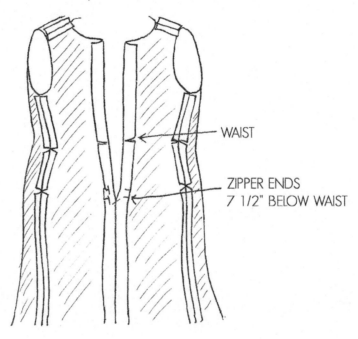

WAIST

ZIPPER ENDS
7 1/2" BELOW WAIST

9. Sew a 22" Zipper at CB. An Invisible Zipper or Lapped Zipper can be used:

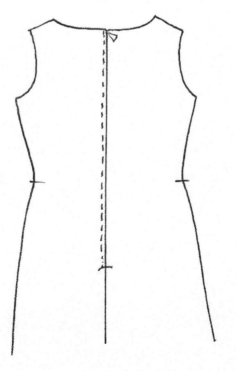

Sculpted Wrap Dress
SEWING INSTRUCTIONS

10. Sew HEM of the dress using a 1/4" baby hem. When hemming the front pieces, once you get to the side seam, clip and turn over carefully. Press the hem:

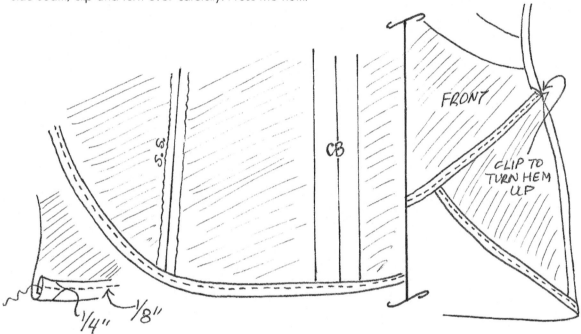

11. Sew the armholes using a 1/4" topstitch similar to the hem:

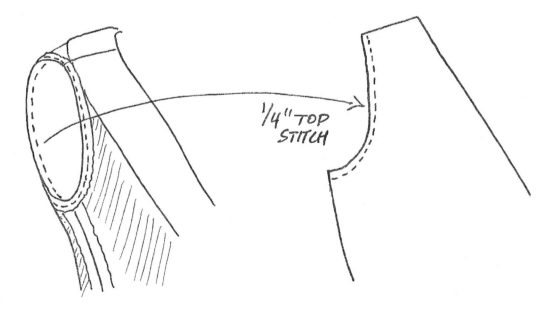

Terminology

APEX: The apex is the highest point of a bust on a dress form or person.

ARM PLATE: The arm plate is an oval metal plate on a dress form that represents the arm's circumference.

BALANCE: Balancing a pattern ensures that the side seams of the garment hang straight on the dress form, preventing pitching forward or backward. When a garment is balanced, it hangs straight without twisting.

BASTING: A basting stitch is a loose and temporary sewing technique used to hold layers of fabric together before permanent stitching.

BIAS: The bias refers to the diagonal line of the woven fabric where the threads of the straight grain and cross-grain intersect at a 45-degree angle to each other. This angle is known as true bias and it is the point where the fabric has the most stretch.

BIAS BINDING: A narrow strip of fabric that is cut on the bias and then folded once or twice. It is used mainly for finishing and for hiding the raw edges of a garment.

BLOCKING: Blocking is when you are manipulating the fabric so the cross grain and the straight grain run into each other at a perfect right angle.

BUSTLINE: The line that delineates the bust level. Drape tape is usually positioned at this point to help in the draping process.

CENTER FRONT (CF): Center Front is an established point that shows the exact center of the pattern or garment in relation to the correct center front of the body.

CENTER BACK (CB): Center Back is an established point that shows the exact center of the pattern or garment in relation to the correct center back of the body.

CENTERFOLD: A step used in draping to prepare your muslin before pinning to the center front or center back of the dress form. This fold is usually 1" and creates a sharp clean edge while draping.

CLIP OR CLIPPING: A small cut made into the muslin while draping to release strain and help the fabric lay flat and achieve the desired shape.

COVERSTITCH: A coverstitch is a hemming technique that creates two rows of stitching on the top and a serger-like stitch on the back, resulting in a professional finish. This hem is mainly used for knit fabrics as the coverstitch allows for stretchability.

COWL: A draping detail that creates a loose fold or folds in the fabric. Cowls are most commonly used at the front or back neckline but can be created on other parts of a garment. Typically, when draping a cowl the fabric is cut on the bias.

Terminology

CROSSGRAIN: Fabric is comprised of threads that run parallel (weft) and perpendicular (warp) to the selvage. The crossgrain refers to the threads that run perpendicular to the selvage.

CROSSMARK: A mark(s) placed on a drape that indicates the position where pieces are to be matched or joined.

DART: A design feature used to take up excess fabric of a defined width and taper it to nothing at one or both ends. This assists in fitting the garment over body curves.

DRAPING TAPE: Draping tape is used to mark out the style lines on your dress form. Common types of draping tape are twill tape, strips of muslin/fabric, or actual adhesive tape made specifically for draping.

EASE: Ease refers to the additional space in a garment beyond the body measurements. The amount of ease added to the drape or pattern helps define the look or style of the garment.

EDGESTITCH: A row of stitching that runs along the very edge of a garment, usually 1/8" or less from the edge. This type of stitching provides a clean and professional finish for facings, collars, pockets, or any area where you want a clean look along a seamed edge.

FACING: A small piece of fabric, separate or a part of the garment fabric itself, used to finish the fabric edges. Facings are mostly used to finish the edges in necklines, armholes, hems, and other openings. A facing is often backed with an interfacing fabric to give it strength and stability.

FLARE: A flare is a style or drape that increases in volume and creates a wider shape.

FRENCH CURVE RULER: A ruler that is used to draw and replicate curves of various shapes and sizes. Most often used to draw the curved lines of a neck, sleeve, bust, and waist.

GRAINLINE: The grainline is the direction in which the threads are running through the fabric. The straight grain is formed by the warp threads, which run parallel to the selvage. The crossgrain, on the other hand, is formed by the weft threads. Understanding and identifying the grainline of a fabric is important for proper cutting and sewing.

HIP CURVE RULER (VARY FORM): The hip curve ruler is necessary for shaping garment contours along the hip line, pant inseam, lapel, and sleeve amongst others.

INTERFACING: Interfacing is a material, either woven or non-woven, that adds stability to certain parts of a garment. It is applied as an extra layer on the inside of garments like collars, cuffs, waistbands, and pockets. This layer helps to add shape, structure, and support to the garment. Interfacing comes in a variety of weights and can be either fusible or nonfusible.

L-SQUARE RULER: This two-piece ruler is in the shape of an L and is most often used to create scaled patterns. For draping purposes, the L-Square Ruler is often used to create perfect 90-degree angles.

Terminology

MARKING: After creating the desired design through draping, the muslin is marked on the dress form to indicate important points like seam lines, darts, and necklines.

MUSLIN: Lightweight cotton fabric with a plain weave made from bleached or unbleached yarns. Its weight can vary from fine to heavy. Designers often use muslin to drape and create their sample garments.

NOTCHES: A marking on a drape or pattern indicating where garment sections should align and be sewn together, as well as identifying different parts of the fabric or pattern.

OVERLOCK STITCH: An overlock stitch is a type of sewing stitch that is used to edge, hem, or seam one or two pieces of fabric. The machine used for overlocking typically cuts the edges of the fabric as it is fed through. The stitch itself is created by interlocking 3 or 4 threads.

PATTERN PAPER (DOTTED, MARKING, ALPHA, ALPHA NUMERIC): A white paper printed with a one-inch grid pattern of dots, numbers, or points. It is used to develop and make patterns and markers.

PEPLUM: A peplum is a short flared or gathered piece of fabric attached at the waist of a jacket, dress, or top which creates a hanging flounce.

PLEATS: A permanent fold that is created by folding one part over the other, sewing across the top end of the fold, and stitching it in place.

PRINCESS LINE: A garment with a seam line that traditionally runs from the armhole or the shoulder to the hem, where the bust and waist darts are incorporated into this seam.

PUNCH HOLE (DRILL HOLE): Punch/Drill holes are used in the fashion industry to indicate where to taper the dart. They are placed a set distance from the end of the dart.

SEAM ALLOWANCE: A seam allowance is the space between the edge and the stitching line of the fabric.

SELF-FACING: A self-facing is part of the actual garment, folding over and connecting without a seam, unlike a traditional facing that is sewn separately as a finishing piece.

SELVAGE (SELVADGE): An edge produced on woven fabric during manufacturing that prevents it from unraveling. Straight grain or lengthwise grain is in the direction of the warp threads, which run parallel to the selvage.

SLASH & SPREAD: The Slash & Spread method is used to create volume and change the shape of your garment or drape. It is also used to manipulate darts by placing darts in other places.

SLEEVE CAP: The sleeve cap is the top section of the sleeve that encompasses the upper portion of the sleeve to the bicep area.

Terminology

SQUARE NOTCH (POINTED NOTCH): Square and pointed notches are traditionally used for knit garments. Square notches are used to signify Center Back and Back Armholes, while pointed notches are used to signify Center Front and Front Armholes, as well as the Waist and other key locations.

STAYSTITCH: Stay stitching is a line of single stitching sewn through one layer of fabric. It prevents the fabric from getting stretched or distorted.

STRAIGHT GRAIN: Straight grain or lengthwise grain is in the direction of the warp threads, which run parallel to the selvage of the fabric.

STYLE LINES: A style line is any seam line other than the shoulder seam, armhole seam, or side seam. A style line is typically used for visual effect and can also be utilized to shape and structure a garment.

TOPSTITCH: Topstitching is a sewing technique in which one or more rows of stitching are sewn on the outside of the garment, either for decorative effect or functional reinforcement.

TRACING WHEEL: A tracing wheel is a patternmaking tool with small pointed spikes, that allows you to transfer pattern markings to the fabric or pattern paper.

TRUEING: The process of blending markings and crossmarks made during the draping process to create a seamless transition. Trueing ensures continuous seams, style lines, and dart placements.

UNDERBUST: The area directly below the bust at the ribcage is called the underbust, also known as the empire line.

WAISTLINE: The line or indentation that defines the narrowest part of the waist.

ZIG ZAG STITCH: A zigzag stitch is a side-to-side stitch that is commonly used for seam finishing, decorative purposes, and sewing stretch fabrics.